Wrong Family: A Memoir

By Charisse Dahlke

For Every Secret, There Is a Family

D1738376

For my sisters,
Teresa, Lisa, Josette, Angelique

September 25, 1984

Dear Charisse,

I was very glad to get your letter. I suppose your mother and stepfather thought they were doing the right thing by not telling you of me, though I don't agree. As to the birth certificate, it must be a phony as I was there when you were born and me and your mother were married at the time and your name was Charisse Elaine McFarlin. I don't even think your mom knew Joe Orona then, who I presume is your stepfather.

I know your sister Teresa's father, he was supposed to be a friend of mine. You are tall for a girl, 5'8", but I am 6' tall and am the shortest one. One brother of mine is 6'5" and one is 6'6".

There are 10 kids of which I am the oldest and the only one not married, and have 27 nieces and nephews. My one brother, Mike, died 7 years ago, he was 24.

I have a friend who works for a moving company and I had him look for you twice when he went through Tacoma, but no luck. I was going to put an ad in the papers out there and go out myself. I knew I would see you someday.

When your mother said I didn't want you when you were little, she is mistaken. I just had no choice in the matter.

I would like to meet you and would come out there if you wanted or send you the money to come here as I know my mother and dad would love to meet you and your son Matthew.

I guess I will close for now as it is 3:00 in the morning. I work 3 to 11 at night. Hope to hear from you soon and I will call you. I have a phone now.

Love,
Gene McFarlin

I

1970: Charisse (Age 7)

Chapter 1

My father brought home a WWII generator so we could have electricity. He ran a long orange extension cord from the shed to the side of the house, where he fed it through a gap between two logs of the A-Frame he had built the summer before.

I primed the engine, like my father showed me, and pulled the rope several times but couldn't get it to turn over. I pushed myself up onto a stack of wood so I could get both feet on the generator as leverage. I pulled as fast and hard as I could. Still no luck, so I tried a few more times until the heavy smell of gas told me to stop. Last time this happened I was worried the shed would blow up, so I walked down to our neighbors. Lynne wasn't home, but Julie said. "You probably flooded it," and then… "Why the hell is a 7-year-old messing with a generator?"

I missed electricity, which had allowed us cartoons on Saturday Morning and The Wide World of Sports on Sunday night. It seemed like such a long time ago that I'd watched the neighborhoods of Tacoma disappear as we drove across the Tacoma Narrows Bridge to start a new life on 5 acres in the thickly wooded rural community of Key Center. Whenever we crossed the bridge, I yelled, "Feet Up!" and all of us girls held our feet up and held our breath so we wouldn't drown. This was a superstition I either made up or overheard, kind of like, "don't step on a crack or you'll break your mother's back."

My dad decided that we would leave it "all" behind for the opportunity to start over. "The fresh air will be good for you girls." All five of us watched out the windows as we left the main highway and followed the water until we crossed a much smaller bridge over the Purdy Spit. "Feet Up!" I yelled again. As we crossed you could smell the salt and mud of the oyster piled beaches. People stood in their waders and thick coats at the water's edge, digging for clams.

The fog was thick and as we drove through it. I imagined we were driving into a cloud and, when we came out the other side, it would be warm and sunny. Instead, we drove further and further away from civilization until the roads got narrower and narrower and then the misty grey sky was replaced by dewy green. The giant fir trees grew closer together on both sides of the road and met in the middle far above our heads. It smelled like Christmas.

You had to know where to turn into our driveway because there were no signs and the brush was always threatening to grow over. There were no streetlights, so in the dark we had to drive very slowly and back-up if we passed it. The only access to the property was on amateurish roads carved out by tractors or bulldozers owned by the people who lived at the ends of these roads. "People who live out there are hiding from something," my grandmother told me when I complained about being so far away from anything.

We had two neighbors. The closest were my mom's cousin Lynne and his wife Julie who lived on the adjacent 5-acre piece. He was the one who talked my parents into moving there in the first place. Bob and Beverly Garlic, a large couple with a tiny baby, lived at the end of the road on their own 10 acres. There were no addresses where we lived, so if you wanted mail, you had to have a Post Office Box in Vaughn, the nearest town. Land must have been cheap, because we were as poor as dirt since my dad either quit or lost his job.

Bob Garlic drove his tractor up and down our long dirt road at least once a month clearing the brush that seemed to grow overnight, threatening to isolate us further from civilization. Bob worked in an electrical construction job, and he would give us giant cable spools that we could use as a table or turn them on the side and race them down the hill. Bob wore the same dirty blue coveralls every day. It was hard to tell what Bob really looked like. His thick, dark beard covered most of his face, so you couldn't even see his lips when he spoke. His head was covered by a brown wide-brimmed hat along with brownish shoulder-length hair that met his beard. He was always busy around the property building, fencing, planting or clearing.

His wife, Beverly, seldom left the property but was always busy doing something around the place too. They lived in a single wide mobile home that had been expanded by attaching wood structures on three sides. When you walked in the front door you couldn't tell it had been pieced together—it seemed watertight. There was a big pot belly stove sitting right in the middle of the room with wood and kindling stacked halfway up the wall behind it. They had stuffed a big couch and two big chairs into the small area, leaving little empty space. There was a hall leading to their bedroom, where there was no door, and the oversized bed came almost all the way to the door. I wondered how they got it in there. In a small alcove, they had managed to stuff in a dresser and an old-fashioned sewing machine.

They had a cow for milk, chickens for eggs, and a large garden where they grew most of their food. Lynne told us that Bob Garlic was really D.B. Cooper. "I swear I saw him dig up a satchel behind his chicken coop, take something out, and bury it again."

I was never sure if he was kidding or not. When I asked my dad about it, he said, "D.B. Cooper was a lot thinner."

In sociability, Beverly was the opposite of her husband. Where Bob didn't speak very much, Beverly was open and friendly. She liked company, so she didn't mind when I came down to visit. She was a large woman with a wide smile and big rosy cheeks. She kept her long blonde hair piled up on top of her head in a messy bun or in a long braid at the back of her head, like a horse tail. She made all her own clothes using that old-fashioned sewing machine that worked by using your feet to pump the gears into action. I enjoyed watching her sew as she moved the fabric through the needle and pumped her feet in perfect rhythm, swish-swish, swish-swish, hands moving back and forth picking up pieces and feeding them into the machine, the whole process like casting a magic spell until all movement stopped and she was holding up an entire shirt.

I liked spending time with her and it seemed like she enjoyed my company. I would watch the baby when she went to milk the cow or collect the eggs. She taught me how to crochet my very own red slippers. She would show me the stitch, let me try it and pull it out when it wasn't right. She gave me a size J hook and some extra balls of yarn she had left over from other projects. These small balls of yarn were my most valuable possessions and I kept them with me.

Our only other neighbors were Lynne and Julie. Lynne was more like a brother than a cousin to my mom. He was a large chested man—as loud as he was big. He had wavy blond hair and big rosy cheeks. His big work boots made him seem even taller when he had to duck under the front door frame. He and my mom were practically the same age and grew up across the street from each other. Lynne had actually lived with my mom and her family for a time in his teen years. My sister Teresa even had Lynne as her middle name. He might have been at her birth or something—I wasn't sure. Teresa hated her middle name because she was named after a boy.

Julie was also a large presence, like Lynne. She was almost as tall as her husband with short brown hair and big brown eyes that looked bigger because of the big round glasses she wore. She was the reasonable, responsible one, so if you had a serious question you would ask Julie—definitely not Lynne.

Lynne's and Julie's cabin was an A-Frame like ours but seemed more like a real house with a bedroom and bathroom. They had shiny wooden floors and a kitchen, where we had plywood covered with a few scatter rugs. They had a well and a septic tank, so they had running water and an inside toilet. We both had wood stoves to heat our houses, but they had brick along the back wall and underneath the stove. Lynne showed us girls how to find water using a divining rod. We spent hours walking around our property holding our special sticks watching for any small movement towards the earth, indicating water. We marked these potential water holes by stacking a pile of rocks in a circle so we could dig a well someday. We even dug one of these holes a few feet deep, using a pick and shovel, but gave up when no water appeared.

The forest that surrounded our small, one room A-Frame was our whole world. We built trails through the brush and hideouts under fallen logs until it got dark and my mom would ring a big old cow bell signaling it was time to come in.

Dinner was cooked using a propane camping stove until my father brought home an old-fashioned wood stove he found at an antique store. The wood cook stove took up a lot of space in the cabin but was worth it because my mom could bake apple pies.

At night, we gathered around our mother on the pulled-out couch where she and my father slept. Mom was working on the battery powered radio, trying to tune in the station for tonight's Mystery Theater episode. The kerosene lamp sat across the room on the large cable spool Bob had given us for a table. It started to flicker which meant it needed more kerosene, but we didn't have any.

The radio wasn't going to work. "It's probably out of batteries," she told us. Sometimes mom would tell us a fairy tale she memorized or read us a story from the bible. Tonight, we listened to her own fairy tale of how she met our father. This was her favorite story and we had heard it many times. The story never changed, mom was working at Peterson's Fryer Farms where it was her job to package the giblets—the livers, hearts and gizzards. She was busy at her workstation when she looked up at the 6' tall, dark, handsome man standing in front of her station holding a tray of chicken livers. "It was love at first sight," she would tell us. She wrote her phone number on his apron and when he walked out of the room, she told the girl working next to her, "I am going to marry that man." Two weeks later they were married and lived happily ever after.

After I found out the truth I wondered about the second half of the story, when Jose picks my mother up for a date and notices two baby girls. I was 18 months old and Teresa only 3 months old. I wonder if my father felt sorry for my mother and decided, "Gee, this looks like fun." Whatever happened they didn't waste any time because Lisa was born 9 months later, Josette 18 months after that, and Angelique 15 months after that. Basically, there are six years between all five of us.

Mom and Dad were an unlikely couple. Mom was born in Seattle to two alcoholic parents, so she spent most of her youth with her grandmother. She didn't do very well in school and always thought she was ugly because she was too thin, too pale, and had a noticeable overbite. Her goal in life was to find a good husband and have a "Happily Ever After" life.

Dad grew up in a small town in Texas. His mother died when he was 15, so he had to work hard and help his father with his two younger brothers and a younger sister. He was six feet tall and had a thick black mustache that he would wax up, curling at the ends. He had dark brown eyes and dark wavy hair. My grandmother said he was a negro, but my mother said he was Spanish. He came to Washington with a few of his friends and tried to join the Army, but he had flat feet so they wouldn't take him.

One of my bottom teeth was loose and I had spent the last few days moving it back and forth with my tongue. It was barely hanging on and my mom wanted to pull it out with a wet washcloth like she had with my front two teeth. I showed Lynne how far I could push it forward when he came over that night. "Get a piece of string," he told me.

I didn't have any string, but I had the yarn Beverly gave me, so I handed the tightly bound red ball to him and watched as he took out his pocketknife and cut off about three feet of yarn. He tossed the remaining ball across the floor. I ran after it, carefully winding the loose end up and setting it on the couch.

He tied a loop on one end of the cut piece and motioned me to him. "Open up," he said and fumbled with his big fat fingers in my mouth. I could taste the tar and nicotine left from his last cigarette. I wanted to spit but kept my mouth open until he finally got it tight around my loose tooth. He fastened the other end to the front door handle. He was sitting by the door on one of the fat logs we used as stools. He had a Lucky beer in one hand and quickly slammed the door closed. Nothing happened. Drool started leaking out of my mouth and down my cheek because I didn't want to shut my mouth and couldn't swallow with it so wide open. He opened the door with his free hand and told me to move back, motioning with his beer hand. I took a few steps back, then he swung the door again.

That did it. The tooth flew out of my mouth and landed somewhere across the room. My mom stood watching and shaking her head. My sisters were horrified even though there was no blood.

I went to sleep that night with the covers pulled tight over my head, creating heat with my breath. I couldn't stop touching the blank spot where my tooth had been, obsessed with the metallic taste of the exposed flesh. I could hear my sisters' deep breaths as they slept all around me. I carefully placed my tooth under my pillow like I had with the two other teeth I had lost, but that was in a different house. I didn't have my own bed. I missed the bunk bed where I slept on top and Teresa slept below. There was a sheet, a blanket and a pillow, all orderly and so tightly tucked that when I crawled in, it was like a big hug, the snugness making me feel secure. I remember waking up with a quarter under my pillow exactly where the tooth fairy had come and taken my baby tooth.

I fell asleep imagining a birthday party like the one we had when we lived normally. We dressed up in pretty chiffon dresses—mine yellow and Teresa's blue, but otherwise exactly the same. We had frilly socks and shiny black shoes. There were lots of kids and we played *Pin the Tail on the Donkey* and *Musical Chairs*. We always celebrated our birthdays together since both of us were born in November, only 12 months apart. We were practically the same size and, since my mom usually dressed us the same, we pretended we were twins. Since we lived in the woods we never had a party and never got a cake, but we didn't complain. When I woke up the next morning, I didn't find a quarter. My tooth was still there.

Chapter 2

My job was to bring the firewood up to the porch and stack it next to the front door. I loved the smell of cut wood and would sometimes put my nose so deep in the wood I could breathe in the aroma as I carried it in my arms from the shed. My father had constructed the small shed, where most of the wood was being "seasoned." Every day my dad would head out into the five acres of forest behind the cabin early in the morning, chainsaw in one hand, gas can in the other. We could hear the familiar weeee and buzz of a thousand bees muffled only by the thickness of the woods. After he had cut the logs into identical sections, he hauled them out into the clearing in front of our porch where he used the wide stump to set the pieces end up and split each one with an ax.

We girls would stack them like puzzle pieces so they took up the least amount of space while allowing enough space to have airflow to dry the wood out so we could sell it. When we ran out of covered space in the shed, we had to stack it around the clearing. My dad would place old pallets side by side so we could get at least a cord or two stacked in one place. Once they were high enough, we covered them with the blue tarps we had used as shelter when we were building the cabin.

I could build the perfect fire, stacking the wood like a teepee on top of balled up newspaper and kindling. The key was to not ball up the paper too tight, use the smallest kindling and then bigger, and not to stack the wood too close together. Sometimes, if the wood was too wet, my father would throw gas on it to get it going. The one time I tried to use gas, I almost burned my hair off.

Everyone said my mother was beautiful and that she looked too young to have five kids. She said her eyes were hazel but they just looked blue to me. She had long red hair almost down to her waist and never put it up or tied it back. She kept it loose and flowing like a big red wave.

"I should have been a dancer," she said. "These are dancer's legs." She did have long, thin legs. She showed us girls how to dance gracefully pointing our toes and curling our fingers just so. She would have us practice our posture by balancing objects on our head as we walked across the room. She named me after Cyd Charisse, a famous dance partner to Fred Astaire.

"Who was Teresa named after," I asked.

"Teresa Brewer, she was a famous singer in the 50s," she said.

"Lisa?"

"A friend." I didn't think my mom had any friends. Poor Lisa, she got the most boring name.

Josette and Angelique were named after characters from "Dark Shadows," the day time soap opera with angels, witches and vampires. It was like a cartoon but with real people. When we had a television we always watched "General Hospital" and "All My Children." Sometimes when we are at Grandma's house we could get caught up in the episodes.

Mom didn't like to be left alone so we always had to stay downstairs with her until our dad got home. Sometimes he didn't come home until the middle of the night so we just moved our blankets to the floor and slept there instead of in the loft. Like most nights, we were all gathered around our mother on the pulled-out couch listening to the stories on the radio and playing gin rummy while waiting for our dad to come home when a loud noise made us all jump and get silent. We could hear scraping and moving. Whatever was out there was bigger than the cat. "I think it's a bear," my mom whispered.

"What if it comes in?" Lisa said.

"It's not going to come in," she said, but the look on her face wasn't matching her confidence. "I think we need to scare it off by making noise," my mom said. "Just start stomping and screaming as loud as you can."

We all got off the bed and gathered around my mother and, on cue, we all jumped up and down, screaming and hollering as loud as we could. When my mom stopped, we all stopped and quietly listened. My mom took the big flashlight and opened the door just a crack to peek out the door. When she was confident enough she opened the door about halfway and moved the flashlight around the front clearing and back to the front porch where the large white ice chest was tipped over and its contents now strewn everywhere. "Good thing there wasn't much in there," she said.

While she was close, still searching the woods with her light, I leaned out and grabbed a few pieces of the split wood that I had stacked earlier, close to the front door. There was a strong odor outside. It smelled like a combination of spoiled hamburger and my dad's really stinky boots. My mom said it was the bear. "You can always smell a bear before you even see one," she said.

I was glad there was still wood there. I didn't want to take a trip to the shed and run into that stinky bear. We always knew that there were bears in our woods. My dad said he had seen them before so he kept a knife with him whenever he went into the woods to cut wood. I kind of wished I would have seen it for myself, but knew I wasn't that brave.

I opened the small door of the potbelly stove that sat in the corner to keep us warm at night, and placed one of the split sections into the bright red embers. There was still a piece that hadn't burned all the way yet, so I stacked the other two pieces on the floor next to the stove. I closed the small door quickly but a few embers snapped, escaping to the floor in front of me. I was barefoot so I didn't step on them but kept my eyes on them, making sure they died out and didn't start a fire on the wood floor.

My eyes were still down when I heard a crash next to me. There was a pot of soup on top of the stove. My mom had set it there after dinner so it would be hot when dad got home. Somehow Angelique had used the wood I had stacked as a step and was able to reach the handle. Now the two-year-old was covered in hot soup, screaming bloody murder.

Mom grabbed her and pulled off her clothes. "Get a towel," she yelled. Teresa handed her a towel and my mom pushed it back at her. "Get it wet." Teresa laid the towel on the floor and poured some water from the five-gallon container we filled at the service station and used for water. Mom wrapped her in the wet towel like a little baby Jesus and held her in her arms, rocking back and forth until she calmed down. She finally set her back on the ground, carefully pealing the wet towel away to inspect the burns. Angelique, calmer now, stood naked and helpless while my mom turned her in a circle. Her left arm and part of her stomach on the same side were bright red but weren't blistering. The rest of us girls stood quietly watching the whole event. Tears stung my eyes but I didn't cry. I felt like it was all my fault.

The next morning, we could see the damage to the ice chest. The bear had ripped the top right off and left gouges either from its teeth or sharp claws. My mom said it was probably a "she" instead of a "he" and that she was probably looking for food for her babies. I hoped that was true. The poor little baby bears were probably starved. I was pretty hungry too, especially now, since she took all our food.

"If we find a baby bear, can we keep it?" I asked.

"The mama bear would probably not like that very much," my mom said. I kept the idea planted in my head so I could think about a way to make it happen. It could be our adventure. We could build a large pen and trap it. We would have to pick a lot of berries before we captured it so it wouldn't starve.

Teresa, Lisa and I each poured a cup of water from one of the clear five-gallon water jugs my dad filled at the gas station in town. This was a two-person process even if the jug wasn't all the way full. One person leaned it over and the other person held the cup. We stood in a line at the edge of the front porch looking down at my mom, who was picking up the scraps of paper and a few cans of beer that had spilled out of the tipped over chest. Josette was standing down in front of us helping her.

We dipped our toothbrushes in our cups to get them wet and then dipped them in the yellow box of baking soda to brush our teeth. The soda was sort of salty and sour, so we brushed fast, brushing, taking a sip of water, then spitting off the porch. Josette was standing just close enough if we aimed just right, we could spit on her. It took a few great aims before she realized what we were doing and moved out of range, giving us all the evil eye.

From Angelique's small arm, my mom unwrapped the bandages she had made from a pillowcase the night before and took off her nightgown. We watched her open one of the cans of beer she had retrieved from the ground and pour it over the red parts of her skin. Whenever we had a cut or scrape, my mother would pour beer on it. If we got a bee sting or mosquito bite, she would combine meat tenderizer with the beer, creating a paste to paint on the bumps with her fingers.

"Will you go to the bathroom with me?" Josette asked, still standing below us moving back and forth trying to avoid our spit.

"I have to go too." Lisa said. We often went to the outhouse together, figuring there was safety in numbers—especially now that we knew there was a mama bear somewhere out there.

The out-house was shabbily built of thick plywood and had black tar paper stapled to the roof to keep most of the rain out. It was never painted and had a roughly cut hole as a window in the back wall designed to create some kind of air flow. It had a platform with a hole covered by a wooden lid where you sat to pee or poo. We took turns standing guard at the door, keeping an eye on the bee's nest that hung low in the left corner under the roof. The bees stayed docile unless you shut the door too hard.

"Are you still there?" Lisa called out to us. She was always scared we would leave her. Whenever you needed to go potty or empty last night's bucket, you had to hold your breath as long as you could in order to avoid the stank. It would stick in your nostrils long after you left the area, so we stood back closer to the path. Sometimes we would just squat to pee behind a tree to avoid the smelly torture.

"I need a leaf." Lisa said loudly, so Teresa quickly looked around and found some leaves and handed them in to Lisa. The maple leaves that were still on the tree were the best because they were soft. Ferns were soft too, but fell apart too easily.

When we got back to the clearing, dad had the truck backed up as close as he could to the shed. We had a good system to load up the truck. We formed a line, passing wood from the seasoned stacks and handing the wood up to our father, who stood in the back of the old grey ford until it was stacked full. The pitch from the logs made my hands look diseased. The only way you could get the sticky substance off was to rub your hands in the dirt, which turned them black. It would eventually wear off but, until then, you had spotted black hands.

Dad took the split wood into town where he would sit by the side of the road advertising it for sale with a big cardboard sign advertising "2 cords/$100." For a small fee, he would even deliver it. Sometimes he came home early with a pocket full of money and a few bags of food. Other times, we were asleep when he came home sometime during the night.

It was a hot day outside the cover of the woods. Mom put on her bikini and covered herself head to toe with a thick coating of baby oil. With two young ones in tow, we all walked out of the cover of the thick woods across the shared dirt road to a bare hill that had been cleared of brush and was in full late morning sun. The hill had a perfectly flat top wide enough for my mom to lay out her blanket. When she was settled, laying face up with small white cotton balls covering her eyes, we took off to the woods, searching for huckleberries and salal berries. The plan was to only eat half— the other half, we would save for the bear.

We didn't get far before we found a large piece of cardboard that we dragged back to where our mom was sunbathing, still face up. The strong sweet smell of the baby oil made me sneeze.

"Can you untie me?" she said, hearing my sneeze. She removed the cotton balls and rolled over, and I reached out to untie her top. I left a dirt mark where my dusty hands had come in contact with her oily skin. "Don't want a line," she said happily.

The hill had been formed when the original road was cut out and now was bare dirt with a few exposed rocks. It was the perfect height and slope to allow us to slide down one at a time using the thick cardboard as a sled. We took turns sliding down the hill, creating mini dust storms as we did. The dust we created was so thick we could barely see each other.

"Am I red?" Mom asked, not opening her eyes. She had turned face up again, with the cotton on her eyes.

I looked at her. "Nope, you're black."

She sat up. "What?" She let the cotton fall from her eyes to see her legs, arms, and belly covered in dust. We were all covered in dust, but it clung to her and was black because of the oil. Her eyes were white from being covered. She didn't get mad. Just shook her head and led us all back across the dirt road to the cabin. "How did I get here? How on earth did I get here?" She kept saying it over and over, "How on earth did I get here?"

Mom moved the big aluminum horse trough with a big #7 stamped on the side to the center of the porch and filled it almost halfway with water from the rain barrel. She boiled pan after pan of water on the camp stove, pouring it into the water until it was at least lukewarm. Our clothes were stripped and piled next to the bath. We took turns washing until we were as clean as we could get. The water had turned black from the very first child plunked into the tub. After we all took our turn, we helped her dump it over the side of the porch, creating a huge mud puddle in front of the stairs that we took turns jumping over.

I also tried to remember what happened to get us here. We had a real house with a real bathroom with a real bathtub. I remember how much fun we had riding our bikes down the hill in front of our house. We pushed Lisa down the hill trying to teach her to ride a bike.

She hit the curb at the bottom and broke her arm clean through. We would also put Josette in the red wagon and told her to pretend it was a car and we'd tell her to steer with the handle. We pushed her down the hill where she crashed about halfway down, sustaining various scrapes and bruises but no broken bones.

I remember my mom pulling that same wagon with the two little ones inside and the other three of us walking beside or taking turns pushing the wagon around the block where we would visit yard sales and we could buy a game or a small toy.

Uncle Lynne stopped by on his way home from work to "have a couple cold ones" with my parents like he often did. Whenever they got together, they drank a lot of beer. He always brought at least a six pack of Lucky Lager in bottles. I couldn't wait until the next morning when I could search around the blackened earth where their campfire had been, gathering all the bottle caps thrown onto the ground the night before. Under each of the bottle caps was a puzzle. It was a rebus where small pictures put together represented a familiar phrase. By the end of summer, I had a pretty large collection and had figured out most of them. I had collected so many, it was rare that I would find one I didn't already have. Occasionally there was one I just couldn't figure out, and I would keep those separate to ask Aunt Julie about later. She always knew the answer but sometimes I still didn't get it.

I could tell my mom was drunk. She was usually the quiet one, but tonight she was laughing too loud and slurring her words. I could hear her clearly because we had made our beds on the floor in front of the couch. It was Easter Sunday tomorrow and we were excited for the Easter Bunny to visit and leave us candy filled baskets. We even left a carrot by the front door as a treat for the oversized rabbit.

My mom opened the door a few inches and looked in on us where we had spread our blankets in front of their bed right in middle of the floor. She saw that we were all fast asleep— except I was pretending to be asleep. I kept my eyes closed but my ears open. "Joe, get the baskets out of the truck." I heard her words clearly.

"I knew it," I said to myself. I got up and went to the wooden door that my mom didn't completely close when she went back out. I opened the door wide just as my father had reached the stairs with five colorful baskets balanced in his arms.

I stood in the open door in front of the stairs. "I knew there was no Easter Bunny," I said. I watched as my mother's wide smile faded. Whenever my mother was upset, she melted into a childlike form. Most of the time I felt sorry for her, so I would retreat or comfort her.

Lynne laughed. "Of course there is, Cheri." He was drunk. "He lives with Santa Clause and the Tooth Fairy." He laughed as my mother tried to recover her composure.

"There is an Easter bunny…" she said in her child like voice, "…but sometimes he comes early so the parents have to hide the baskets until the kids go to sleep." I watched Lynne roll his drunken eyes as my mom's wide eyes warned him to shut his mouth, but he didn't.

"That is a good one, Bernice." He stood unsteadily. "What are you going to tell her when she finds out about her invisible father?" I stood small in the doorway in my pajama's starring at the adults with confusion. I looked at my dad who stood frozen mid step, still balancing the colorful baskets.

"What about my father?" I looked from my mother to my father. My mother didn't seem drunk any more. She had moved to my father and now stood behind him. She wasn't going to look at me. "What is wrong with you?" I asked him.

"Go to bed," he told me. My father closed the door and I could hear my mom crying loudly. I couldn't hear the words because they had moved and were speaking in hushed tones, but I knew it was bad. I heard a bottle crash against the side of the house. I wasn't sure what I said that was so bad, but I was terrified to open my eyes as my parents carefully and quietly set the Easter baskets near our heads.

I never saw Lynne again.

Chapter 3

"Mommy and daddy won't wake up." Lisa was shaking me. She was crying, and the other two little ones sat up next to her in a sleepy daze. Since we all slept in the same bed, when one kid woke up, everyone woke up. Teresa and I slept at the top and the three little ones at the bottom, legs intertwined on each level. Teresa and I got out of bed and started calling for our parents.

The loft was quickly filling with smoke, but it was still so dark it was hard to see each other. I don't remember how we all made it down the ladder, but we did, and got out the front door. It was partially blocked by the wood stove that my father had already moved so he could reach the source of the fire where the yellow and red flames were licking at the wall of the cabin behind the wood stove. The chimney hung suspended from the ceiling above his head.

We stood on the front porch away from the door and the black smoke. My dad walked past us with buckets of water he was getting from the rain barrel while mom was using an old wool blanket to hit the flames that had moved to the floor. "Get in the truck," my dad yelled to us.

We crawled up into the cold blue front seat, watching the scene unfold through the fogged windshield like we were at a drive-in theater. My mom crawled up into the truck with us, still holding the blanket she had used trying to smother the fire and covered us as much as she could.

I was tired and so cold I was shivering and I could feel my teeth chattering. "Can we please go to bed?" I asked my mother.

"There is still too much smoke. We need to let it air out," she said.

"I'm cold," said Lisa, who was sitting closest to the door next to me.

"Sit on Charisse's lap," Mom told her, and I moved my legs so she could sit and fit under the blanket. Small droplets of rain silently appeared on the windshield. Combined with the fog created by our breath, a blurred world isolated us from the outside.

Our dad finally opened the door of the truck, letting in the cold fresh air, and got in with us. Without a word, we automatically arranged ourselves in the same configuration as we did when we went anywhere. Dad sat behind the steering wheel. Mom sat next to him with Angelique in her lap, Teresa held Josette and I held Lisa. My legs were tingly, falling asleep, so I shifted and woke up Lisa who had her head against the cold window. My dad had brought an extra blanket that smelled like smoke, so we all had covers now.

I didn't cry but wanted to feel sorry for myself. I conjured up a familiar memory of a time when I had skinned my knees tripping over a bump in the sidewalk at our old house. I just remember my knees hurt so bad I had tears running down both cheeks and snot running out of my nose. I had long sleeves, so I wiped the snot on them until they were drenched. When I found my mother, she was too busy changing Angelique's diaper and Josette was in the highchair screaming for something. I tried to get my mother's attention and followed her into the kitchen where she hurriedly put some peanut butter on a slice of white bread as she balanced the baby on her left hip. Josette just continued screaming when my mom walked over with the peanut butter bread and smashed it right in Josette's face. Josette quit screaming and I went out the back door wiping the snot from my face with my already wet sleeve. I sat on the back porch picking out small rocks from my bloody knees, still crying because I felt like I didn't even matter, that if I got run over by a car, no one would even notice.

The next morning, our little house in the woods proved to have only a little damage as a result of the fire, but my dad couldn't start the fire because he had to put the stove back in place and fix the stove pipe. The whole house smelled like burnt toast. It really wasn't that bad. Teresa and I found our clothes and got dressed for school. We were both tired since we didn't get much rest with our sisters sleeping on our laps. We looked forward to the long warm bus ride to school.

I loved everything about school, but the best part was going to the library. It was my child heaven. I loved the smell of the paper and ink. I loved to walk down each isle reading the spines, sometimes moving the books in and out so they could be perfectly lined up. I liked the order of the card catalog and the Dewey Decimal System. I loved that I could check out books whenever I wanted. Laura Ingles Wilder was my favorite author because her stories reminded me of our life, but instead of on the prairie, we lived in the woods. I would read to my sisters or tell them about the stories so we could act them out. When my parents took us to the property in Key Center, I was excited when they described how they would build a cabin. It was just like in my books.

No matter where we lived, school was my sanctuary. Whatever was happening at home didn't matter. School was always the same no matter what school it was. The day always started with bells and announcements, standing for the *Pledge of Allegiance*—sometimes I even got to hold the flag at the front of the class—recesses and lunch, and the end of the day always happened at the same time every single day. I liked how predictable it was.

My third-grade teacher was a tall, thin older lady with short grey hair that smelled like flowers. She had light watery blue eyes that were framed with fancy cat's eye glasses that had three little diamonds on each side. I thought she must be rich to have diamonds on her glasses. Her voice was soft but stern. Even when she was mad or trying to get the class's attention, she spoke in a sing song voice, only louder. When the boys ran around the classroom like monkeys, she would raise her voice, "Okay boys, let's settle down." Sometimes she might ask twice, but if the boys didn't settle down to her satisfaction, she would silently leave the class, returning with the principle, who would take the boys out to the hall. The boys came back to class, sometimes with tears in their eyes, rubbing their behinds, and sat quietly in their seats.

The desks were lined in five rows of six desks each. There was only one extra desk at the very back that had no student sitting in it. I secretly wished we would get a new kid in class and it would be a girl. I would make sure I would be her friend so she wouldn't feel awkward. I would let her walk around the playground with me and Teresa and I would show her the library.

We were assigned seats in alphabetical order by our last name, so I was seated in the fourth row near the back. I wished I could sit up front but really didn't care where I sat as long as I got to be in school. I loved everything about school except recess and lunch. Math and Reading were my favorites. I raced to be the first one done with my math assignment and begged for any extra worksheets. I look back and realize that the hunger for learning has never left me.

The teacher walked down the rows handing out worksheets. She stopped at my desk and stared at me for a few seconds before moving on to the next student. I quickly filled in my name with a capital "C" and a capital "H" and the rest lower case "arise." I don't know why I did that. The instructions were to fill in the appropriate word from a list below. These were easy, but I completed it as fast as I could by using perfectly formed cursive writing. Cursive was not required on this assignment, but I was an overachiever.

She had barely made it back up to the front of the class and turned around when my hand shot up, but instead of calling on me she motioned me up to her desk. The rest of the class was still working on their worksheets.

"Do you have a question?" she asked me in a voice just above a whisper to not disturb the other students.

"Can I have another worksheet?" I asked.

"Is something wrong?" she asked me as she looked me up and down like she didn't even hear my question. Her watery eyes got smaller like she was trying to read my mind or something. Then she smiled her normal smile and reached out to move my hair out of my eyes. I followed her action with my own hand and moved the other side of my hair out of my eyes and smoothed down the back part which might have been sticking up. I hadn't brushed it. I usually had a big knot of hair hidden underneath the back of my head that frustrated my mom whenever she had tried to brush it out. I didn't have the patience to get the tangles out so I normally brushed only the top parts.

"Nothing is wrong. I'm done with my sheet and just wondered if there were any more." I handed her the completed sheet I had brought up with me.

She hesitated for an uncomfortable few minutes still trying to burrow into my brain. But my brain was blank, so she finally said, "let me see what I can find." She took off the glasses and let them hang from the chain around her neck as she opened the bottom drawer of her desk, picking out several light-yellow file folders. She looked at me again curiously from head to toe. I followed her eyes as she examined me. My pants were too short so my dirty ankles were exposed. I had forgotten to put on socks. She pulled out a few sheets from each folder and handed them to me.

"Thank you," I said, turning to go back to my desk when she put her arm out blocking my path.

"Did you go to a campfire last night?" she asked me. "You smell a little bit like smoke."

"No," I said. "Our house almost burned down," I said, like it was really no big deal. I really just wanted to get back to my desk so I could work on my pages.

"What do you mean your house almost burned down?" She still had not moved her arm. We were playing a soft game of tug a war.

"Sometimes sparks fly out of the stove because there is so much pitch in the wood or just too much wood," I told her. "We just had to wait for the smoke to clear before we could go back in."

"Did you call the fire department?" she asked. A few kids in the front few rows were now paying attention, hearing a reference to a fire department.

"No. We don't have a phone. My dad put the fire out with the water from the rain barrel." I told her. "It didn't even burn through the wall, but he put a tarp over the roof just in case." I had watched him secure the blue tarp as we walked down the driveway on our way to the bus. He used bungee cords and ropes, making a big covered area between the house and the wood shed.

"Why didn't he just use a hose?" she asked.

"We don't have a hose. We are saving up so we can get a well. Then we can get a real bathroom too," I told her, holding the papers protectively against my body.

"What do you drink with or cook with?" she cocked her head in such a way I thought she thought I was lying.

"We fill our water jugs at the gas station," I said, a little frustrated. She finally moved her arm, giving me an open path back to my desk.

I had barely sat in my desk when the recess bell rang. "Go out to recess, now," she told me, noticing I wasn't moving out of my chair. I was disappointed but I obeyed without question. I opened my desk and set the pages on top of all the desk items. I was the last one out the door, and she followed me out, locking the classroom with a key that hung around her neck. I watched as she walked toward the main building.

The chaos of the playground was disturbing to me. Kids ran around screaming, kicking balls, and playing hopscotch. I found my sister sitting on a bench watching some girls playing 4-square.

"Wanna play on the monkey bars?" I asked her. We both had calloused hands from hanging and twirling on the cold metal bars during our recesses.

"I am too tired," she said. I sat next to her. I was tired too.

The bell rang but neither my sister or I ever went back to our class room. Instead, one of the office ladies came out to the bench where we sat and led us into the main office where we were told to wait. The only time I had ever been to the office was when my mom first brought me to the school to register. We sat in the hard-plastic chairs for what seemed like forever, leaving only once to use the restroom. The restroom at school was like going to a park because of the large concrete sink that sat in the middle. It was like a fountain that spit water only when you stepped on the metal ring at the bottom.

I always took a long time washing my hands, stepping on and off the ring, imagining crawling into the large sink and letting the warm water run over my whole body including my head. The bright pink soap was slick and smelled so good. I pulled up my sleeves and washed all the dirt and soot from my hands. I looked into the mirror noticing my un-brushed hair and it was kind of sticking up on one side. I put a little water on it and combed through with my fingers until it laid flat. Before I left the restroom, I went into a stall and plucked out a few squares of toilet paper, folded them and stuffed them in my pocket.

I went back to the seat I had been put in earlier and sat next to my sister. Teresa had moved and was sitting sideways on the chair and had her head leaning against the wall. I think she might have been asleep. She had kept her coat on even though it was warm in the room. The office was busy with people moving in and out. A few sick kids were taken to the nurse's office until their moms came and took them home. There was an office lady messing around a big fancy looking machine that sat in the middle of the office. She told me it was a mimeograph machine. It made copies.

"Can I help?" I asked her.

"Sure," she said with a smile on her face. She let me dip the thin metal spatula into the can of thick black ink and fill the trough along the roller. She took the metal spatula from me and with a quick motion evenly spread the ink. She attached a stencil and let me turn the handle. I was thrilled as the copies spit out one after another. I breathed in the smell of the ink. It almost smelled like gas. Teresa and I always rolled down the windows at the gas station, even if it was cold, so we could breathe in the smell of the gas. I decided I would be an office lady when I grew up and I could make copies all day.

I was so consumed with the mimeograph, I didn't notice the woman in a brown suit walk into the principal's office until she came out and was now standing next to me.

"Miss Orona?" I heard her say it but was wondering if she was talking to me or my sister. Nobody ever called us Miss before. I looked around the room but she was looking right at me. I could feel my cheeks get flush but I didn't know why.

I looked at Teresa who must have also heard and had moved herself back to a front facing position. "Can I speak with you for a few minutes?" I shrugged my shoulders but didn't speak. She moved aside and opened her arms towards the open door to the principal's office. When I moved toward the intended direction, she took a few steps to my sister and took her small hand and brought her in behind me.

The principal had a big smile on his face. I had never been in this office. There were certificates hanging in frames with his name on them. A few pictures of his family were scattered around on his desk, but the most interesting item in the room was hanging on the side wall. It was a long handled wooden paddle with holes drilled through it. This must be what the bad boys in my class were hit with when they didn't behave.

"Why don't you girls have a seat over there." He pointed to a small orange couch directly under the paddle. I looked up at it as I sat near my sister.

The lady took a chair from in front of the desk and moved it so she was right in front of us. She sat with her legs crossed, clipboard in hand and a pencil that she kept twirling in her fingers. Her glasses were low on her nose and she looked at us above them. Her blonde hair was pulled tight in a perfect bun on top of her head with two perfect curls hanging from each side right in front of her ears.

"My name is Mrs. Jones and I work for the Department of Child Welfare," she said with her pencil now standing straight up, primed to start writing. "I heard you girls had an adventure last night."

"It wasn't an adventure." I said. "It was a fire. An adventure would have been exploring or going somewhere like going to the circle." My sister nodded her head because she knew the difference.

"What is the circle?" she asked and put her pencil to the paper waiting for my answer.

"It's where we go on adventures."

"We?" she asked

"My sisters and me."

"How many sisters do you have?"

"Three more," I said, and Teresa nodded her agreement.

"Wow…" she said, "…four girls "

"No. Five." I corrected her and Teresa again nodded her head. "Me, Teresa, Lisa, Josette and Angelique."

She looked at my sister and back to me. "Do you all have the same mom and dad?"

"Yes." I thought that was a weird question.

"Tell me about the circle." She changed the subject back to the adventure. I told her about the path that used to be a road and the big clearing on the property where we girls would play. It had some old appliances that we moved around and old wire rolls that we could sit on and pretend we had wheels or we could stand up and have a table. I also told her we were starting to gather some branches that we would put together as a pen for our pet bear when we found one. She seemed impressed, so I kept telling her stories. Most of them were real. If she watched Teresa, she would know when I was telling more than the truth. Teresa couldn't lie so she would frown when I was exaggerating.

"It's where we stayed while my dad built the cabin," I said—which was the total truth. I explained how it was like camping because we had tarps that my dad and his friends tied with ropes so they were like tents hanging up in the trees and we had a campfire every night. "That was our adventure." She was writing very fast and it was quiet. The principal still sat back in his chair, with both his hands on his pouched belly, just listening.

"Can you tell me more about the fire at your house last night."

"It was just a fire. It didn't burn down. It was mostly smoke."

"Were you afraid?" she asked.

I looked at my sister and then the lady. "A little bit, but we have angels watching over us."

"That's nice…Angels?" I could tell she didn't believe me but she smiled with sarcastic green eyes.

"Teresa saw an angel in our house," I said. At the time, I was sure it was because we said our prayers that night.

"It was right above my mom's head," Teresa added, and I went on to describe the night when Teresa woke up to go to the bathroom because we forgot to bring the bucket up and when she reached the top of the ladder looking down to where my parents slept, there was a ball of light floating in the air right above our mom's head. Teresa wasn't frowning, so the lady could know it was the truth because Teresa never lied.

"There was nowhere the light could have come from. We are in the middle of the woods. It couldn't have been light from anywhere else since we don't have electricity and the stove had already gone out. We didn't have windows so it couldn't be the moon. It was definitely an angel," Teresa said.

The lady looked frustrated and kept looking at the principal who still never moved until the end when the lady said, "I think I have everything I need." The principal stood and walked her out of his office. They closed the door and we could hear them talking in a low voice, so we couldn't hear what they were saying. When he came back in he pulled his coat off of the back of his chair and told us he was taking us home. I wanted to ask if I could go get my papers from my desk but I was too scared.

We didn't go to school the next day or the day after that. I begged my mom to let me go to school. "We are switching schools," she said. I was sad. I liked my teacher and I really wanted to get those papers. She gave us each a black garbage bag. Josette put it over her head thinking we were going to use the bags as raincoats like we had done whenever we had to walk too far in the rain. My mom pulled it off her head. "Go pack your clothes."

We went upstairs and put our clothes into the bags. We didn't have too much so it didn't take us long. We threw the bags down to the couch out of the hole. Josette held on tight to her dirty faced life-size doll, Maud, who she had dressed in one of her own shirts. It was too big for the doll, so Josette tied a piece of rope around her waist, making it look like a dress. I brought a ball of yarn and the set of jacks I had in my pocket. My dad said he would come back for the rest later.

"What about the cat?" I asked my mom. Kiekie wasn't the cuddly kind of cat that would curl up on your lap, he was the type that barely tolerated humans. My dad had found him and his sister at the dump when he was just an itty-bitty kitten. Dad couldn't capture the sister but somehow got Kiekie trapped and brought him home. When Angelique saw him, she said Kiekie instead of kitty so that became his name. My mom wouldn't let him come in the house but let him hang around because he killed mice.

Kiekie was a huge black cat with half an ear and a scar on his face from fighting with wild animals in the woods. At some point, we realized he wasn't a normal cat because when he hissed he was really loud and he showed us all his big sharp teeth. He must have liked us because he always brought us presents of squirrels and other small animals that he killed and dropped right in front of the cabin door. One time we opened the front door and Kiekie had brought us a snake but he didn't kill it all the way so it came in the house. My mom put a white five-gallon bucket on top of it. When my dad got home he chopped it right in half with a shovel. It left a big red blood spot on the floor right where we slept sometimes. I was glad we were moving.

"The cat will be fine," my mom said. "It's wild."

1905: Nels Saint Clair (Clara) (Age 18)

Clara's father stuck a knife in his right eye trying to remove a button from his shirt. Steven was an unfortunate man that was followed by the devil. Even when he worked on the presidential campaign for Abraham Lincoln in Indiana, he was forced to flee when his name was plastered on posters all over town as a traitor. He joined the Union Army and served several years until his poor health landed him in the hospital where he was discharged with a small pension in 1865.

When he returned home he found his wife had died and his six children had been dispersed to the farmers in the area. He really couldn't afford to take care of them anyway, so he moved to Nebraska. Still suffering from the digestive and abdominal problems that forced him out of the army, he had to find another way to make a living but he also needed a wife to take care of him.

He married Alice, a woman 40 years younger than him, and had three more children. Unfortunately, only one was a boy, and they could barely keep up with all the work on their 160-acre homestead. His health continued to worsen until he could no longer work and he had to sell the farm.

Clara was the eldest of the two daughters and was born when her father was 64 years old. Della, her sister, was two years younger and already married. The family finances were dismal, so at 18, Clara moved to Hood River, Oregon, with her brother who became a cook at a logging camp and she became a Flunky. Flunky's were the girls hired to assist the cooks at the logging camps. They worked from early morning to late at night making sure the loggers were well fed.

Clara met Walter, a rough but handsome man, five years older, but who seemed a little immature for his age. Women were scarce at a logging camp, so Walter worked hard to gain her favor. It wasn't long before Clara found herself pregnant and in 1905 she and Walter were married in a small ceremony. Clara sent word to her mother about the baby, but by the time the letter arrived, Alice had died from a sepsis infection. Clara was devastated and was inconsolable until the baby was born. She named the child Della after her younger sister but held the small child in her arms for only a few months before the child also died.

II

1971: Charisse (Age 8)

Chapter 4

It was the day before Christmas. We had laid out blankets in the back of the station wagon so we could sit or lay down on our trip to Texas to meet Dad's family. My mom stuffed a large brown grocery bag under the seat before we folded them down into the flat surface. I figured it was our Christmas presents since we wouldn't be home.

It took about four hours to get to the bridge that took us from Washington to Oregon, and in another hour my mom pointed out the sign that said Eugene. "That is where Grandpa White lives," she said.

"Can we go there?" I asked.

"Not this time," she said. "We have a long drive all the way to Texas."

Grandpa White was my mom's real father that we couldn't talk about to Grandma Nelda. Grandma told her whole family that her first husband had died in The Battle of Pork Chop Hill during the Korean war so we had to keep it a secret that we knew him. One time, I accidently said something about "Grandma Green" in front of my Grandma Nelda. My mom said it was an old family friend of my dad's.

It was raining most of the time until we got to the pass, and there was snow piled up on both sides. Driving through snow was quiet. The noise the traffic made was muffled like we were driving through a cloud. Big trucks were pulled to the side putting chains on, but we just kept going. We got through it all with just a few slips and slides along the way.

We watched the cars and read the signs. We played silly games and told stories. I brought a book, but every time I tried to read it I felt like I was going to throw up. We spent the night at a rest stop and ate bologna sandwiches on white bread with miracle whip. If we had to go to the bathroom, my dad pulled over to the side of the road and we stuck our small butts out the window, or if there was enough room we could get out and squat.

"How is Santa going to find us?" Lisa asked my mom. It was dark now and we all knew that it was Christmas Eve, which meant Santa was supposed to come down the chimney. I already knew there was no Santa but played along for the other girls.

"Santa knows everything. He knows if you've been good or bad," my mom said.

"Look, there's Rudolph!" I yelled, pointing up to the dark sky. There was a flashing red light far above us. I knew it was likely a satellite, but the girls were convinced it really was Rudolph's nose and soon fell asleep hoping for a visit from Santa.

My dad stopped at a gas station to fill up, and when he went to pay he bought five red netted see through Christmas stockings filled with a variety of nuts, chocolate and a small orange. My mom pulled out the grocery bag from under the seat and set out five small identically wrapped packages. I listened to everything that was going on, still pretending to be asleep.

By the next morning, we had reached the Texas border. My dad had driven all night, at one point stopping for a small nap. My mom handed us each a bologna sandwich and told us we could open our presents. We each received the same exact plastic toy, which I can't even remember, but it would be the type of thing you would find at a dollar store today.

We opened the stockings, each with a price tag of 99 cents, and ate the orange and chocolate. We couldn't eat the nuts, except for the peanuts, because they were in a shell and you needed a nut cracker or a hammer. By the end of the trip, the unshelled nuts became a hazard. They got out and were everywhere. Every time you laid down or sat up there was a walnut in your back or under your butt.

The first stop in Texas was my dad's grandparents' house. It was late afternoon and we were all just very glad to be out of the car. Angelique had no shoes, so we had to take turns carrying her around. Dad's grandpa came out of the small grey house like a giant. His head almost hit the cover of the porch. He put on his cowboy hat that had been sitting atop the old fashion washing machine that looked as if it was still being used on the front porch. Next to the house there were clothes hanging on a line moving with the breeze.

It was warm there, and we were all still bundled up wearing the same clothes we started out with in Washington State. We stood in a line next to my mother, who was currently holding Angelique, two on each side at attention like small soldiers ready to greet our relatives.

As tall and slim as Grandpa was, Grandma was extremely short and wide. At eight years old, I was as tall as she was. She was dark-skinned with lots of wrinkles even on her hands. The grandfather was lighter skinned. I had never seen anyone so tall in my life. He wore a wide brimmed brown cowboy hat and grey snakeskin cowboy boots that only added to his height. Even though he was dressed like a cowboy, he looked more like an Indian with his serious brown eyes and long eyelashes, along with his light brown skin, sharp nose and high cheekbones.

Neither of these Texas great-grandparents spoke English so we communicated with smiles and hugs. My dad translated a few things he felt might be important information for my mother, but otherwise we all just stood quietly observing the back and forth between them. The grandmother took my mom's arm and led us into the small house. It looked like a living room, kitchen, bathroom and bedroom arranged in a perfect square. It was made of some kind of concrete that had been painted white at one time but since had flaked off in places. There was a window in each room and a tall fan in front of the window in the living room creating some air flow. I was so hot, I could feel the sweat run down my back.

Great-Grandma had a beautiful smile that was so wide, you could see the gold fillings in the back of her mouth, her eyes were so dark brown, you could barely see where her pupils were. Even though we couldn't speak to each other, we felt very welcome. She sat next to my mom on the small couch. Teresa, Lisa and I sat on the floor in front of my mom like we usually did when we were at someone's house. Grandma reached out and touched my hair and smoothed it. She said something in Spanish which I assumed was a comment on my hair since she continued to touch it and smooth it like it was some magical straw you could weave into gold.

We didn't stay long but there were lots of hugs and grandma tears as we left for our next stop. Dinner was at Dad's cousins house. Most of the people who gathered spoke both English and Spanish but everyone had brown hair and brown eyes. There were two kids about my age, a boy and a girl. Both spoke English but with a Texas type southern drawl so you still had to listen carefully when they spoke. The house was so big I was afraid to go to the bathroom because I might get lost. They even had a swimming pool in the back, so it was kind of exciting that we could go swimming on Christmas day.

The boy's name was Emanuel and he was my age. He brought me into his room. He had a single bed centered under a large window that had curtains with blue and red trucks matching a rumpled comforter on his bed. The walls were white with blue trim and there were two pictures of old fashioned trucks like the ones on the bedspread and curtains. Everything matched, but the room was messy. He had so many toys and books there were piles on the bedroom floor. I could hardly contain myself. I started picking up the mess and organizing it so I could see everything. He had a small bookshelf without books, they were spread out all over the floor. Emanuel helped me but got distracted with a box of baseball cards. He sat on the bed and I stacked books on the bookshelf.

With all the big stuff out of the way, I found a card a little bit bigger than a playing card that had "9 X 4" written on one side and "36 / 9" on the other side. I kept digging through everything until there was a full stack of multiplication and division cards. I was so excited to find them all. I sat next to my new cousins on his bed and flipped through them over and over. The answers were printed in small red numbers on the opposite side but I didn't even need to cheat.

"You can have those if you want," he said without looking up from his baseball cards.

"You have to ask your mom," I said calmly, but I really did want to keep these. I followed him into the kitchen where the adults had gathered and he asked his mom and she said sure. She was short like most of the women here and had jet black hair and beautiful light brown eyes. She spoke regular English but could switch to Spanish right in the middle of a sentence. I was wondering if I would see my dad's aunt, the one my mom said had blonde hair and blue eyes like mine.

There was Spanish music playing in the background and lots of unfamiliar smells created by whatever was cooking in the big pots on the stove.

I watched my dad's cousin lift the lid to the largest pot on the stove and I jumped back not believing what I just saw. It was a small grey animal with a pointy nose. It looked like a giant sleeping rat.

"It's an armadillo," Emanuel said noticing the horror on my face.

"You eat that?" I asked.

"I don't," he said laughing, "but its tradition."

"Thank God. There is no way I am eating that either." I still had my new cards in my hand. I wanted to put them in my mom's purse but I wasn't sure where she put it.

People kept arriving and the house was so full people had to gather outside. They brought coolers filled with beer. Everyone was having a good time, laughing and dancing. I never heard my dad speak so much Spanish. The only time he usually spoke Spanish at home was with Uncle Hector when he didn't want us to know what he was saying and sometimes when he was talking on the phone to his sister or his dad. Every once and a while he would try to teach us Spanish by only speaking to us in Spanish but since we didn't know what he was saying, he quickly gave up and spoke in English. One time we found a set of albums at a yard sale. A man with a deep voice would say a word in English and then Spanish. We would repeat after him but nothing really stuck in our heads, so we just gave up.

My dad's mom, Machala, died from stomach cancer when he was 15 years old. It was sad because my dad had to stay home from school to take care of her because his dad had to work. I think that is why my dad treated my mom like she was so fragile. I think he was scared she was going to die.

My grandfather didn't remarry until all four of his kids were out of the house. He came to Washington before we moved into the cabin. I remember he would teach my mom how to make Mexican food that my dad liked. Uncle Hector and Uncle Cruz were teenagers then and I watched them roll cigarettes on the back porch.

I never liked Mexican food until later in life when I found out it didn't have to be so spicy. My mom overdid the chili powder and the jalapenos whenever she cooked a Spanish meal. I would make such a fuss, she let me eat cereal. If there was no cereal and I was hungry, I would mix the rice and beans together to drown out the taste of chili pepper in the rice. Onions must have been cheap because she put them in everything. I hated onions and would pick every one of them out of my food.

Grandpa Orona was an older version of my dad, tall and thin with wavy jet-black hair and a straight sharp nose. He had remarried a few years after his visit to Washington and now had a new wife and two small children. His wife, Lupe, was the same age as my mom and not as friendly as my grandpa. She was thin and had sharp features like the oldest of their two boys. The younger boy was close to Angelique's age. They called the older one Wee-Wee but his real name was Jerry, and the other one Little Joe.

"Little Joe?" I whispered to my mom. Since my dad's name was Joe and he was a junior, how could this kid have the same name? "Can you name two kids the same thing?"

"I guess so," she said. I was still trying to work it all out in my head.

"Are these kids our uncles?" I asked my mom. She nodded yes.

I whispered to Teresa, "Those kids are our uncles." We both giggled.

The front door opened and Uncle Hector and Aunt Yolanda walked in together. I was surprised because they both lived in Washington with us.

"Where is Aunt Rena?" I asked Uncle Hector.

"She is with her mom," he said. He looked sad or tired, I couldn't tell, but it was unusual for him to be so quiet and low key. His mood soon improved when Uncle Cruz walked in. They started yelling Spanish to each other, which was probably teasing since their smiles got wide and everyone around them smiled.

"Somebody get me a beer," Uncle Cruz yelled. It was Grandpa who handed him a beer.

"This is the first time all my kids have been together since Joe left Abilene in '64," Grandpa said as he joined his first set of children. He put his arm around Aunt Yolanda, his only daughter, and kissed her on the head.

I sat next to my mother on the couch with all my sisters gathered around. We were the outsiders to this group.

"Did you come to Texas?" I asked my mom.

"This is my first time," she said.

The next day, the adults were all hung over. We had slept on couches and floors but we didn't care, we were just so tired and glad to be out of the car. The Christmas tree stood lifeless in the corner of the living room. A few bulbs had fallen off and tinsel was all over the floor. There were snowflake decorations that seemed so strange since the sun was shining and everyone was wearing shorts. We didn't have shorts but my mom cut off the bottom of our pants to make shorts so we could go swimming in the pool.

Later that day we all packed into someone's car and headed for the store. Everybody had somebody in their lap. I don't remember who was driving but they decided to take the corner a little fast to catch the light. I was squished in the middle so I didn't see everything that happened but the back door flew open and a small body rolled out into the middle of the intersection.

Luckily, the light we were trying to beat changed and all the cars in each of the four corners were stopped. The small body was that of my sister Teresa. I saw her get up and stagger to the sidewalk where she was met by my aunt. My mom was freaking out crying, "Oh my God! Oh my God!"

Teresa wasn't crying. She stood dazed, "Terry, Hun…" Aunt Yolanda stood in front of the small girl and spoke to Teresa in her heavy southern accident. "Y'all I think she is in shock." She inspected her body for broken bones before she picked her up and brought her back to the car that was now parked next to the sidewalk where Teresa stood. She had scrapes on her legs and arms but nothing more serious.

"At least her face is okay," my mother said. We all changed places until there was room for Teresa to sit on my mom's lap.

We left a few days later to go back home. I was tired of hearing Spanish and eating spicy food. I wanted to go home. Aunt Yolanda rode back with us because uncle Hector was going to stay longer so he could see his "almost ex-wife." I don't think I was supposed to know that but I heard him tell Aunt Yolanda who southerly said, "Hector, don't y'all get yourself kilt."

I missed Aunt Rena. She was a true Southern Belle. She told us that she and Uncle Hector were high school sweethearts. In her yearbook, there was one whole page with her picture as "The Queen" and the other side was a full-page picture of Uncle Hector that said, "The King." She reminded me of Cinderella dressed in a poofy chiffon gown and with a heavy southern accent. Uncle Hector was handsome and popular in high school. He was 5 years younger than my dad but they both were the same height, they had the same straight nose and thick wavy black hair. You could tell they were brothers.

Whenever Teresa and I got to spend the night with Uncle Hector and Aunt Rena, she would show us her yearbooks and point out all the pictures with her and Uncle Hector. She taught us how to play *Clue* and *Monopoly*. She told us that she was a spiritualist and could read tea leaves and read cards. She even had a Ouija board that she showed us how to ask questions.

"Is Hector drinking beer right now? "she asked the board. We all three had our fingertips lightly touching the planchette. It moved slowly to the left of the board on the word "Yes."

I wanted to ask more questions so when Aunt Rena got bored she left Teresa and me alone to play.

Teresa asked "Does Lisa hated us?"

"Yes," it answered and we giggled.

"Is our dad getting a new job?" I asked.

"Yes," it answered.

"Will I get a Chrissy Doll for Christmas?" Teresa asked.

"Yes," it answered. She was excited.

"Am I adopted?" I asked.

"No," it answered.

"Am I adopted?" Teresa asked.

"Yes," it answered.

Chapter 5

The Ouija board was right about my dad getting a new job. He was working somewhere on the tide flats, which was the stinky part of Tacoma. We found a house close to where we used to live before we moved into the cabin. Boeing was the biggest employer but was going through massive layoffs so only half the houses on our block had people living in them. The empty houses with overgrown grass and piled up newspapers were too spooky and I imagined they were full of ghosts that watched out the blank windows as I walked by.

Our house was small. It only had one bedroom so my dad hung two bedsheets, like curtains, between the dining room and living room and set up a king size bed where all of us girls slept. At night, we would take turns watching the TV from the gap in the center of the curtain when we were supposed to be asleep in bed. We were not allowed to watch night time TV because it "wasn't for kids."

It didn't seem like anything bad. It wasn't like going to the Drive-In Theater when my parents put us in the back of the truck with blankets. There was a canopy with two side windows so we would take turns watching. It was Lisa's turn to watch and someone got their head cut off. She started crying and we panicked, trying to calm her down because we didn't want to get in trouble for watching.

The little house wasn't too far from Main Street and there was a small park only a few blocks away, with swings and a merry go round. One day I was running to the monkey bars where Teresa and Lisa where twirling and tripped in a small hole. I fell and couldn't walk so my sisters ran home to get my mom who found a neighbor to take us to the emergency room.

I broke my leg and had a cast all the way up to my hip so I couldn't go to school. I could barely go to the bathroom, my mom had to hold me up to the toilet. My teacher sent my homework home with Teresa so I wouldn't fall behind. My dad even brought me some books, *Tom Sawyer* and *Little Women*.

When I was able to go back to school it happened to be Valentine's Day and I was surprised when I had a bag full of valentines from the classmates I barely knew. I couldn't wait to get home and read each one, but because I missed so much school, I couldn't remember where my bus stop was so I got off at the wrong stop. I watched the bus turn the corner a few blocks away when I realized I didn't know where I was. Nothing around me was familiar. It was a typical February day in the Pacific Northwest, so the sky was covered in dark clouds and there was a light drizzle.

I put my valentines stash under my coat to protect them from the rain. It was a busy street and cars passed by not even noticing this tiny girl walking aimlessly in an unfamiliar town. I walked to where I saw the bus turn and decided my house had to be somewhere in that same direction. My feet were wet and cold. My hair was soaked and was now glued to my head. When I turned the corner, there were more storefronts I didn't recognize. I started to cry and the tears were hot on my cold wet cheeks, my valentines slipped and hit the ground, spreading them across the wet sidewalk. I gathered them as fast as I could but they were now struck together. I put them under my coat again hoping to fix them later.

I walked block after block, pausing at each corner and examining each road for anything familiar. I must have gone five or six blocks before I decided the street I was on had potential so I followed it a few blocks and I realized I was on the other side, so I cut through the alley and found my backyard. I was soaked and feeling sorry for myself when I walked in. My mom was cooking something on the stove and didn't notice me walk in. She probably never noticed I didn't come home on the bus with my sister. I put all my valentines on the heater vents until they dried. I took off all my wet clothes and put my pajamas on. I sat on our big bed reading each of my valentines, trying to put a face with the name signed on the back.

We moved again but this time it was a lot bigger house with a lot of property. There were fruit trees everywhere, apples, pears, and plums. The house was red and was shaped like a barn. We slept upstairs. There was a gap on one side of the stairs that someone had covered with a thin piece of plywood. We would take turns jumping across it to a small alcove on the other side.

My mom was down the street at a neighbor's house when Teresa made the jump and landed in the middle of the plywood. It didn't hold and I watched as she fell in slow motion to the floor below. I flew down the stairs and saw that her eyes were wide open but she wasn't breathing.

"Help!" I yelled. "Please help." No one was home. My other sisters were with my mom. I didn't know what to do. I needed to save her but I didn't know how. I ran out the door and across the field to find my mom. I pounded on the door.

"She is not breathing," I said.

"Who?" my mom asked.

"Teresa," I said. My mom ran and I followed but when we got to the spot where she had fallen she was sitting up with tears running down her face.

She looked straight at me. "You left me," she said.

"You weren't breathing," I said. "I didn't know what to do."

"You probably just got the wind knocked out of you," my mom said, helping her stand up.

We never jumped across the gap again even when my dad put a heavier piece of plywood across it.

A few days later we decided to pick apples. They were ripe and my mom promised to make apple crisp. There was a wooden ladder but it was broken on one side. We stood it against the tree but we couldn't reach the best apples at the ends of the branches, so I found an old metal rake in the shed. It was rusty and old but good enough to scrape the apples out of the tree. I tried it and got two apples.

"I want to try," Teresa said, so I handed her the rake. She was really good at it. She found the apple she wanted and patiently fitted the prongs around it, pulling gently to release it from the tree. Josette and Angelique stood by below the tree racing to retrieve the fallen fruit. We had a bucket halfway full when Teresa successfully pulled another apple from the tree but when the rake came down, Josette's head was in the way and the metal prongs poked right through and blood started running into her face. She had several holes in her head.

We took her to the house where my mom cleaned her up and examined her head.

"Get me a beer," she said. I ran to the kitchen and brought her a beer that she popped open and poured over Josette's head as she leaned over the tub, then she wrapped her head with a towel. Teresa felt so bad that she sat with her that afternoon. I went out and got the apples we had already collected. Lisa had the rake now with Angelique standing below collecting.

"I think we have enough," I said, inspecting the ones they put in the bucket and throwing a few out that had worm holes.

It was Christmas Eve and I was not looking forward to Christmas morning. I didn't believe in Santa and knew we were too poor to get presents. My parents got some free presents from someplace. I overheard them talking and when I snooped under their bed I saw the packages. One had a tag that said, "Girl age 8 to 10."

We were all gathered around the small window upstairs looking into the sky and searching for Rudolph's nose. We were so close to the window that our breath combined with the cold outside kept fogging it up and we would have to wipe it off. We finally gave up and went to bed.

I'm not sure who woke up first but we all woke up and ran downstairs as quietly as we could. It was barely light out but we could see there were lots of presents under the tree and our stockings had been filled to the brim. Because I had snooped, I thought I knew exactly what presents went to who but there were unfamiliar packages stacked on one side of the tree. They were perfectly wrapped in shiny paper with ribbons and bows on each one. I examined them carefully, finally finding a card attached to each one in an envelope with our names written in fancy cursive writing.

"How did these get here?" I said out loud.

"Probably Santa," Lisa said.

"I don't think so." I picked up one of the packages I recognized from under my mom's bed and it had different writing that said "from Santa" and had no ribbon and no bows.

The little girls had their stockings emptied in front of them, separating candy into little piles. My mom and dad came out of their bedroom still sleepy eyed. My mom went into the kitchen to get the coffee going and my dad sat in the high back chair near the tree.

All of a sudden, I heard some heavy steps above my head. Someone was upstairs. We all froze, listening to the creaking of the wood floor. There was definitely someone up there.

"It's Santa," Lisa whispered with wide eyes. I looked at my dad to see if he was alarmed at the obvious intruder. He just smiled, so I was confused. We all watched the feet, legs, arms and body come slowly down the stairs until a face we hadn't seen in a long time appeared like Christmas magic. It was Uncle Hector.

"Merry Christmas," he said loudly. All five of us girls ran over and surrounded him, hugging him wherever we could fit our arms around.

"When did you get here?" Teresa asked.

"I think I got here right after Santa Claus. I'm pretty sure I saw the reindeer take off from the top of the roof," he said. I rolled my eyes and he winked at me.

"Are these from you?" Josette pointed to the stack of fancy presents.

"They are," he said as he sat on the couch in front of my dad.

"Who wrapped them," Teresa asked.

"My wife."

"You have a wife?" I asked.

"What does she look like?" Lisa asked.

"She is a small Chinese woman. She doesn't speak much English." He said it so seriously I couldn't tell if he was kidding or not. I looked at my dad and he just shook his head so I figured he was joking.

III

1972: Charisse (Age 9)

Chapter 6

My grandparents lived on a few acres in a small rural community down a long dirt road. Across the street was my grandma's sister. Edith had three children, two from her first husband, Lynne and Artha, who were both as old as my mom, and she had one daughter, named Bonnie, from her current husband. Bonnie was just a few years older than me.

My mother grew up on Golden Given Road in a small shack next door to her grandmother. But after my mother and her sister moved out, Grandma and Grandpa moved into a single wide mobile home. They didn't do any maintenance to it so it's original brown and white was now dirty brown and mossy green.

We drove into my grandmother's driveway and could see her sitting out on the front porch. She stood and waved and we could see she had no shirt on. She was just wearing a bra out in the open. I looked at my dad's face to see if he was embarrassed but his face didn't change. We all piled out of the truck and ran to my grandmother.

My father started unloading the few boxes he had in the back of the truck, stacking them in the barn behind the house. My mom took our black garbage bags of clothes into the small spare room. Grandma set up the sprinkler in the front yard and we took off all our clothes except for our underwear to run through the sprinkler. She giggled and ran through a few times with us. Grandma was less than five feet tall, so I was taller than her. She had dark black hair and big brown eyes. She wore cat's eye glasses and bright red lipstick that made her look like she was always smiling.

She actually did smile a lot, especially in the afternoon when she was drunk. She danced and sang and told us funny stories.

It was late afternoon so grandma had already started speaking in her German accent even though she was born and raised in Seattle and wasn't German. She was a character and we loved being around her. She could play any instrument by ear. Her favorites were the organ, where she played her hymns, and her guitar, where she would strum out the old Western songs.

Grandma Nelda always had a cigarette in her mouth so, whenever she was nearby, it was best if you kept the cigarette in view so you wouldn't get burned or ashed. When she smoked, she often let the ashes build up instead of tapping them into the ash tray. She also didn't bother to take the cigarette out of her mouth when she spoke, she just talked around it.

We got to celebrate the 4th of July at Grandma's house. Grandpa and my dad put up a badminton set in the front lawn and went to the reservation to get fireworks. We built projectiles with two sizes of aluminum cans and water. The smaller can had a hole for a firecracker. When it exploded, it would fly in the air. We took turns lighting the firecrackers. My dad gave us some to just toss. Teresa held one back and I lit it for her. She tried to throw it but the fuse was too short and it blew up in her hand.

We went into the house and my grandma and mom took a look at it.

"At least you didn't lose a finger," my grandma said.

My mom held her hand over the kitchen sink and poured whatever was left of the beer she was currently drinking over Teresa's burnt hand. Grandma went to the bathroom and brought out some type of salve and spread it over the burned area and wrapped it with an ace bandage.

"It still hurts," Teresa said. My grandma took two aspirin and crushed them between two spoons until they were powder. She mixed the powdered aspirin with sugar and water, stirring it with her pinky until it was fully dissolved.

"Open up," she said to Teresa.

Teresa opened her mouth wide and grandma poured it in.

Living with grandma was fun. She danced around and taught us funny songs like "Bill Grogan's Goat." My parents and grandparents would sit in a circle and strum on four guitars and sing old Western songs. My favorite was "Burning Ring of Fire." Occasionally Grandma would try to teach me some hymns on her organ.

Sometimes grandma let us pick through the dish of hard candy that she kept in a bowl next to her chair. I liked the root beer ones shaped like little barrels. The peppermint always stuck to the other candies, but I didn't mind. If it was raining and we had to stay indoors we sat on the floor looking through the stacks of "wish books" grandpa kept under the end table next to his chair. I took Sears and Teresa took JC Penny's. We would search for our favorite toy or outfit, marking those pages. When Christmas came close, we would use the books to make a list of what we wanted from Santa.

The worse part of living with grandma was that we had to eat everything on our plate, no matter what it was. I didn't like most of the food my grandma made but I tried to eat what I could. At our old house, we would put the food behind the refrigerator that was in the garage. At Grandma's I had to wait until Teresa wasn't looking and put my food on her plate. I sort of felt bad because she would have to sit at the table all night because she didn't finish.

The trailer was small so there wasn't a lot of room for all of us. Grandma and Grandpa slept in their room at the very back of the trailer. There was barely enough room for the bed and a dresser. The bathroom was right next to their bedroom. My mom and dad slept in the other bedroom, which was lined with boxes stacked on top of each other everywhere. The closet door wouldn't shut because it was so full of stuff. There was a narrow path to the bed. All of us girls slept on the floor in the living room.

The house was always filled with smoke from cigarettes— both grandparents smoked one after another. Sometimes they would forget one was already lit and sitting in the bull dog ashtray and they'd light another one. Most of the time we would pretend we lived in the clouds. Grandpa worked at the lumber yard driving logging trucks around. As soon as he came home from work the half gallon of R&R came out of the freezer. He filled up two glasses with ice and booze. He left just enough room for a splash of water.

Grandma Nelda was a story teller, but I was never sure if the stories were true or not. My favorite was the earthquake story, and since I was not even two years old and have no memories before 5 years old, I had to take grandma's stories for truth.

"It was a 6.5 earthquake, April 29, 1965. I was bathing Teresa in the kitchen sink and you were playing with Lady. I remember when it started to shake. Lady led you over to the door and I grabbed the baby out of the bath and my cigarette fell right in the water. It was a miracle. The Lord Jesus was watching over us."

I could imagine the cigarette dropping into the kitchen sink bath half smoked with the ash still attached from the beginning and the bright red lipstick ring on the camel colored filter. I could imagine Lady, the giant German Shepard that I supposedly pulled and pinched at, still saving my small life by leading me under a doorway for the 45 long seconds where pictures flew off walls and furniture moved across the room.

"Where was my mom?"

"She was working."

"Where was my dad?"

"I have no idea."

Nelda claimed to be a devout Lutheran, but I am not sure she ever went to church. Her church was the Midland Tavern almost every day after work or most of the day on the weekends. My mom said that they stayed with her Grandma Nelly most of the time, since her mom was either at work or at the tavern. By the time I was born, grandma didn't work anymore. She lived on disability because of a back injury she sustained working at the retirement home, but she still kept the same stool at the tavern.

We started another new school when we moved in with Grandma. We had to walk down the hill to the end of the road to catch the bus. There were a few other kids that were on our street that caught the bus with us, including our cousin Bonnie who lived across the street. Bonnie's dad had built a shelter where we could stand out of the rain while we waited. Bonnie was a few years older, so we automatically looked up to her. She acted like a big sister and even told us what seats to sit in on the bus.

"She has an attitude," my grandma said about Bonnie, "spoiled rotten, potty mouth, brat."

The worst thing about living with our grandparents was they both greeted us with big sloppy wet kisses directly on our mouths. The smell of whiskey and smoke stuck to you forever. Today, Grandma was more excited than usual. She jumped around like a little kid until she couldn't keep it in any longer. "I got you girls a horse."

There were two kinds of little girls in the world—those who hope for a pony and those who don't want to go near a pony. All five of us were the latter kind. We had no desire to get near a horse. Grandma led us around the back of the house where there was a large doghouse with an old German Shepard chained to a pole. Her name was Lady. She didn't really like to play. She just laid there on her stomach, paws out in front, following us with her eyes, head steady with the only movement an occasional ear twitch.

The back acre of the property was enclosed by a barbed wire fence with the top wired with electricity so the horse would get a jolt if it touched it.

"Don't touch it. You'll get shocked," Grandpa said, and just to prove it, grandpa tried to get one of us to reach out and touch it. Since no one volunteered and we ruined all his fun, he staggered away. Grandma was still excited and turned off the switch to the fence so we would get closer. There was a beautiful, very large white horse with sad brown eyes staring straight at us.

"Girls, this is Sugar. You can ride her whenever you want." I looked at my sisters as they stood back with no interest.

Grandma reached into a large bag and pulled out a handful of oats. She opened her hand flat as Sugar stuck her head over the fence and moved her big horse lips back and forth, eating the oats out of Grandma's hand. She had huge white teeth and a large pink tongue. Sugar moved her head up and down like she was nodding with approval. She made some horse noises asking for more.

"Come on Terry. You want to feed her?" Teresa was the closest, and even though she didn't want to, she moved cautiously to the fence. The rest of us stood like statues, hoping we would not be next. Grandma once again dipped her hand deep in the bag, pulling out a fistful of oats.

"You got to keep your hand flat," she said as she put a small pile in Teresa's open hand. Slowly Teresa put her hand up towards the horse's big face. She squeezed her eyes shut as the horse eagerly moved its lips like she had with my grandma. Instead of moving her hand back, she froze and somehow the big horse teeth took a bite out of my sister's little finger. It was exactly the outcome we all were afraid of. Teresa held her hand as the blood dripped down her arm. Grandma grabbed a tissue out of her pocket and wiped off the blood but it didn't stop bleeding. "That is why you keep your hand flat," she said.

Then she went into the small wooden shed next to the horse fence and grabbed a dirty towel and wrapped Teresa's hand with it. The storage shed is where the boxes of our family's belongings were stored. It was also the laundry room and pantry. There were shelves lined with jars of pickles, jam, and green beans that my grandma and mom canned. There was a big plastic sink and gardening tools. The lawn mower was also stored in there and filled the small space with gas fumes.

The last time I went into the shed, I was looking for a book my mom said was in the boxes when Grandpa came into the shed, blocking the door. He was unsteady on his feet and I could smell the booze and cigarette smoke even through the gas fumes. I stood and he hugged me tight. I hugged him then tried to pull apart when he put his gross, smooshy lips on mine and tried to put his tongue in my mouth. I pushed him back and ran out to find my mother.

My mother was sitting on the bed in her room and I sat on the bed with her. I was shaking in disbelief as I told her what had just happened. "Just stay away from him when he is like that," she said nonchalantly. "When you were just a baby, he came over to my apartment and offered me $50 to have sex with him."

"Oh, my God, Mom, he is your dad."

"Step-dad," she said.

"Gross."

Bonnie's house, across the street, was a double wide mobile home in much better condition than my Grandma's. It had a big front porch with overflowing pots of flowers guarding each side of the door, and well maintained flower beds were planted all along the front and sides of the yard. The backyard looked like a huge park with a big wooden swing set and a tree house. She also had a wooden playhouse with a realistic stove and cupboards full of miniature silverware and dishes. There were yellow curtains with tiny pink flowers hanging in both windows. The little front door had a pink heart painted on it. The little girls were in little girl heaven, so they stayed outside and played in the playhouse and Teresa and I went inside with Bonnie.

Bonnie loved horses and had a collection of horse figurines that lined the shelves of her bedroom. She took one at a time off the shelves, telling us all the uniqueness of that particular horse. Neither of us cared but faked our interest with a nod of the head at appropriate moments. She also had some big puffy ribbons hanging around the room, some red, some blue, that she said she had won with her horses. Her horses were penned at the back part of their property. Sometimes I watched her ride down the dirt road in front of grandma's and, with a quick tug of the reins, disappear into the woods on a small trail. She seemed to have the giant beast under control at all times.

I was leaning over at the side of grandma's house picking rhubarb so my mom could make a pie, when Bonnie appeared from the woods on her horse, scaring me to death. She laughed and I turned red.

"Don't stand behind her, or she will kick you in the stomach and you might die." I took her warning seriously and didn't get anywhere near the horse whether she was riding or leading it around.

Sometimes, she came over to Grandma's to ride Sugar. "You have to ride a horse often or they won't let people ride them anymore," she said. She would wash and brush and braid the mane of the giant horse like it was one of her small plastic figurines.

I only rode Sugar one time and it was with my grandma leading us around. She lifted me up in the saddle and put my feet in the stirrups and we walked around the property a few times. The entire ride I felt sorry for the horse. I feared we would hurt the horses back or I would fall off.

Mom called Bonnie a free spirit. Her parents let her wear make-up and short skirts. Since she was the youngest child, she pretty much did anything she wanted and got whatever she asked for. I wasn't jealous, just in awe. We would sneak off to the back woods where she would smoke. She offered me cigarettes but I didn't really want to smoke. I tried once and coughed so hard I felt like throwing up.

Grandma would take us for a ride to town and we would stop at the tavern and wait outside in the car while she went in to talk to a friend. To keep us busy, she would bring us treats of peanuts, popcorn, and sometimes ice cream, from the gas station next door.

Clarence was one of Grandma's friends from the tavern and was the person who sold Sugar to Grandma. He was a short old man, a bit bent over as he walked, with a shock of grey hair that he didn't bother combing. He had a sharp nose and small watery eyes, reminding me of a cross between a Christmas elf and the troll that lives under a bridge. His crooked fingers were stained where he held his cigarette. He smelled like booze and smoke just like Grandpa Elmer. Grandma Nelda knew him from the tavern.

Bonnie and I were outside my grandmother's house when Clarence came out of the house and spotted us. He waved us over behind his truck, where he was leaning on the back bumper.

"Hey beautiful." He brought Bonnie into a one arm hug. "Who is your friend?"

"She is my cousin."

"Hi Cousin." He smiled a yellow toothed smile that made me feel uneasy. He reached into his front shirt pocket and handed Bonnie a pack of Lucky Strikes. Bonnie took the cigarettes and quickly put them under her shirt and tucked it in. "How about a little kiss?" He leaned down to her, exposing a cheek, but as she was about to kiss his cheek, he turned to meet up with her lips. I stood frozen, a little confused by the interaction.

Chapter 7

The following Saturday, we loaded up in the back of the truck and followed the grandparents to Clarence's farm. It was across the Narrows Bridge, so we picked up our feet and held our breath as we crossed it.

When we got there, Bonnie and her parents were sitting at a picnic table with Clarence and his wife. There were a few other people but no other kids so we sat listening to adults talking about things we didn't really understand. We finally ate burgers and homemade potato salad and pork and beans. All the adults had drinks in their hands.

I didn't notice Clarence leave the group but when he appeared he was leading a horse towards us. "Who wants a ride?" he looked right at me.

"No thank you," I said.

"No thank you," repeated Teresa.

"I'll give you a ride," Bonnie said to Teresa and me. "We will go real slow."

"I will get the other horse. You and this little one," Clarence said pointing to Teresa, "get up on this one, and blondie can ride by herself."

Grandpa helped Teresa get on the back of the horse behind Bonnie and told her to hang on. There was no saddle, just a blanket. Teresa put her arms around Bonnie's waist and the horse moved back and forth a bit. I could tell Teresa was scared by the look on her face. Bonnie galloped ahead just a few yards and turned the horse before the second horse arrived. This one didn't even have a blanket. He was a darker shade of brown and his giant brown eyes watched me closely.

He had a bridle in his mouth that looked uncomfortable and Clarence held the leather strap in his hand. Grandpa lifted me up and told me to hang on to the mane or I would fall off. I grabbed a tuft of horse hair and hung on for dear life. All of a sudden, I could smell horse poop. I wanted to gag but had to focus on staying on top of this horse. Clarence guided the horse forward and we followed Bonnie and Teresa around through a narrow path in the woods, nice and slow. I started to relax a little but concentrated on keeping my balance so I wouldn't slip off either side.

The path widened a bit now and we were out of site of the family when Bonnie took off in a strong gallop and disappeared into the woods ahead of us. Clarence laughed a horse type laugh and dropped the leather straps, then slapped the animal's hind quarters. It took off, leaving the man behind and running through the forest towards Bonnie and Teresa. I could barely hang on and figured there was no stopping this wild horse without getting a hold of the straps hooked onto the bridle. The branches of the trees were too low and they hit me in my face and head. I lay down as much as possible, burying my head into the mane so I couldn't see where we were going. My heart was jumping out of my chest and I was too scared to even cry. The horse slowed down and started to trot back just as we neared the clearing where we started. I don't remember who grabbed the horse or who got me off that horse, but that was the last time I would ever get near a horse.

The scratches on my face burned as the tears rolled out of my eyes. I quickly wiped them away before anyone could see that I was crying. I squeezed in next to my mom and sat there with my head down, humiliated. No one said anything, they just kept laughing and talking, drinking beer and whiskey like nothing happened to me. I had just had a near death experience—I couldn't eat or drink anything in fear I would throw up. My heart was stuck in the middle of my throat. I wished I could have a Nancy Drew book and a hiding place.

The sun went down, the horses were stabled and everyone now sat around a fire pit roasting marshmallows on long sticks. Some people took their time creating an evenly brown crust, some just plunged the stick directly into the fire creating a torch for a gooey black mess.

I was too tired to deal with a marshmallow and I had to keep moving around to avoid the smoke. If I moved too far from the fire the mosquitos attacked my arms and legs. "Smoke follow's beauty," my grandma said to me, noticing my movements.

"Beauty was a horse," Bonnie whispered in my ear. I was starting to move from feeling sorry for myself to getting pissed off. Clarence's small grandma looking wife said we could go inside and watch television, which I thought was an excellent idea. She gave us blankets and opened the couch so we could lay across it like a bed. Bonnie, Teresa and I watched television and snacked on stale popcorn.

At some point, we all must have fallen asleep. I woke up and it was dark except for the glow of the television. I had to use the bathroom so I sat up, trying to focus my eyes in the dark so I could see where I was. Bonnie and Teresa also woke up and Bonnie turned on a side lamp that wasn't very bright but was enough light to show the way to the bathroom. Teresa came with me.

The house was quiet and there was no noise coming from outside. Apparently, our parents had gone and left us there. When we came back from the bathroom, Clarence was sitting on the couch with Bonnie. He handed each of us an oversized t-shirt.

"Here, change into these," he said. Bonnie took her shirt off and put the shirt over her head. "Take off the shorts," he said. His voice was gravelly and he spoke quietly, just above a whisper. I couldn't see his eyes, but his head turned toward my sister and me. "Are you going to change?" he asked.

I don't remember saying anything but took the shirt to the bathroom. There was no lock on the door. I had just pulled my own shirt over my head when Clarence opened the bathroom door and slipped in. Without saying a word, he reached out and took the shirt out of my hand and laid it on the sink, then sat on the toilet and pulled me towards him. Before I could react, he was kissing my non-breasts with his sloppy lips. I shook uncontrollably as he removed my shorts. I now stood before him naked except my underwear.

He pulled me close and whispered in my ear with his stale breath, "Shhhhhh…. don't be afraid." He sat me on his lap where I could feel the hard lump against my leg. He pulled it out and put my hand around it. I held on not knowing what to do. I was afraid to react when he reached in to my panties, exploring places I had never even touched.

"Doesn't that feel good?" he said softly in my hair. I shook my head "no." He laughed quietly and grabbed my small hand, which was still wrapped around the slug like unit, and moved it back and forth until hot sticky liquid was all over my leg. He wiped it off with one of the towels he pulled from a rack. He then pulled his over-sized shirt over my head. I could smell the musty cigarette odor that had infiltrated the cloth—it smelled like him. It came almost down to my knees. I wished it was longer.

He opened the bathroom door quietly and slowly led me back to the couch. "This is our secret, okay?" I nodded slowly.

A few days later, I was sitting in grandma's kitchen with my mother while they were stuffing beans into Mason jars. The kitchen was foggy with all the steam from the oversized pot where they were blanching the beans. There was a vinegar smell that tickled my nose, but I didn't want to go outside. I was sitting at the back of the small kitchen table near the window and my grandmother must have noticed my daydreaming look as I stared at nothing out the window.

"We can go ride Sugar later if you want to Chari."

"I never want to ride a horse again," I said still staring out the window.

"Why not?" she asked. I turned my head towards her slowly. Did she not remember a few days ago when I almost died?

"Because Clarence tried to kill me. He hit that horse on purpose. I could have fallen off."

"You did fine. I was proud of you," she said.

"Clarence came in the bathroom and kissed my t-t's," I said. Both women instantly stopped what they were doing and turned toward me. Grandma grabbed her little tan pouch where she kept her cigarettes and shook one out. As she lit it, the strong scent of butane cut through the fog and she sat in the chair in front of me. My mom took the chair beside her. I could hear the water boiling and the television noises coming from the other room, otherwise there was silence. The two women stared at me and I felt guilty but I didn't do anything.

"What else," my mom said. It looked like she might cry. I recounted what I could remember. I really didn't want to talk about it, especially the gross parts, but I told them most of it.

"Mom, what are you going to do about that?" My mom turned toward my grandmother.

"What do you want me to do about it? Men are disgusting, all they think about is sex. Just stay away from him." She took an extra-long drag from her cigarette and I watched as the long ash fell into one of the open jars of beans. She picked out what she could but continued working on never taking the cigarette out of her mouth until she needed a drink of her tall glass of R&R and Water. "You know what you do next time?" She pointed her head my way looking right in my eyes. "You take a big bite out of that thing."

"Mom!" my mom turned red. I was wide eyed and disgusted looking between these two women who were so different. My grandma was outspoken and energetic, where my mom was soft and quiet. My mom didn't even look like her mother. Maybe she was swapped at birth? Grandma was short and thick with black hair and brown eyes and my mom was tall and thin with red hair and blue eyes.

"Jesus Christ, the man is so old he probably couldn't even get it up," Grandma said, lighting another cigarette and sucking hard and blowing out the smoke that disappeared into the cloud that still lingered from the last one.

"I'm going to say something," my mom said.

"You do that."

IV

1973: Charisse (Age 10)

Chapter 8

Salishan was a neighborhood originally built in the east side of Tacoma between 38th and 56th streets during WWII to provide temporary housing to the people who moved to the Northwest to work in the shipyards and factories where they would build ships and planes for the war. It was now subsidized government housing for people like us. Identical light yellow painted houses lined both sides of the streets in perfect rows. Some were single family and some were duplexes. There were some apartment buildings closer to 56th street. Kids were everywhere, riding bikes, skating or running through sprinklers in the small yards.

Our house was the last one of the row on the corner lot, so we had a large side yard. The small back yard was not really a yard but a slab of concrete enclosed by a six-foot wooden fence. The other side of the fence dropped off into the First Creek Ravine, which we called "the Gulch." It was a deep cavern, probably 20 to 30 feet across and at least 20 feet deep, filled with fir trees and salal bushes. It spanned the entire 20 blocks as a greenbelt.

Three police cars were parked in front of our house with lights flashing but no sirens. Two officers with large German Shepard's were at the side yard next to our house near the edge of the gulch.

"Let's go out and see what's going on," I said to Teresa, who was sitting on the couch brushing her Chrissy doll's hair. Last Christmas, Teresa finally got a red-headed Chrissy doll and I got Velvet, the blonde one. I didn't like dolls, but whenever my mom got us dolls, Teresa got the dark one, I got an identical blonde one and, I am not sure why, but Lisa would always get the black one. Maybe that was the reason Lisa always wanted to have black children.

My mom was sitting at the kitchen table studying her school books. She was going to beauty school so she could get a job as a cosmetologist. As we walked past her I watched her mouth move as she read silently. She said she wasn't good in school, so we had to be quiet so she could concentrate.

We closed the door quietly behind us so the little girls wouldn't follow us. Some of the neighbors were outside across the street also trying to find out what was going on. The police radios spoke and cracked to nobody in the empty cars as the police stood on the edge looking down in the gulch. We walked across the street with the other people standing around. Between two of the houses, I could see my aunt's house. Their house looked exactly like our house except the yard was brown and there were bikes piled in front of the front porch.

"Let's go get Tim and Tim," Teresa suggested, noticing my line of sight. We ran through the houses to the front porch of our aunt's house. The front door opened to reveal a disaster. Toys and clothes scattered the front room. My aunt was cooking something in the kitchen. She was the opposite of my mother. She was short with long dark hair and huge brown eyes like Nelda. It was hard to imagine how they were sisters. My aunt had 5 kids, like us, but her family was blended. She married a man with two boys and she had two boys and a girl from her first marriage. I didn't remember her first husband very much and I didn't like this one.

"The police are here looking for a murderer," I said. I didn't really know why the police were behind our house, but I knew if I said that my cousins would come with us. Teresa was just about to say something so I elbowed her in the rib as a signal. She didn't lie.

My cousins took the bait and got off the couch where they were reading comic books. Len was the oldest and the same age as me. One Tim was my "real" cousin and the other Tim was Len's brother. We called our real cousin Timmy so we always knew who we were talking about. Timmy hated his nickname.

"Let's go," Len said. I had a secret crush on Len and was excited he was going to come with us.

"Who's dead?" one of the Tim's asked.

"They haven't brought up the body yet," I said. "I heard the radio from the cop car. I think it was a rape and murder." I really didn't know what a rape was, but I was sure it was bad.

"I want to come too," Christine said. Christine was the only girl of the family, and we always felt sorry for her because she lived with so many boys and they were always fighting. The only time my sisters and I fought was when the parents were gone, and as soon as one of us started crying, we felt bad and apologized. The boys at my aunts were always rolling around, punching and breaking things.

"You need to watch your brother," Aunt Wilma shouted from the kitchen. Danny was the youngest and a happy, chunky baby who seemed to always have a dirty or snotty face. He cheerfully stood in the play pen babbling at us. I waved at him and he giggled.

"Maybe you can come over later," I said to Christine, hoping it would make her feel better. She had sad brown eyes that were always partially hidden behind her long thin bangs. Even when she smiled, she looked sad.

The boys grabbed their bikes and led the way back through the houses toward our house. We were just in time to see a handcuffed man being dragged up from the side of the gulch. They had two officers holding the side of a tree that was straining to heave another officer from the steep bank.

The handcuffed man was a young black man with a big afro. His hair had bits of leaves and sticks in it like he was hiding under a pile of brush. His eyes were black, and when he spotted us across the street, I was sure he looked right at me. He didn't look like a murderer but more like a scared cat. I suddenly felt guilty, like he was thinking I was the one who told them where he was. I moved to stand behind one of the adults who had gathered.

"He doesn't look like a murderer," said Tim the new cousin. He also noticed the boy was just a scared teen. A murderer would have been much older and evil looking.

Tim's comment started a rumble in our small crowd. "He looks like a murderer to me," said one of the older kids that had gathered around us.

"That's the second murder in the gulch," said another. I was just kidding when I said that to my cousins, but was it true?

That night, I couldn't sleep imagining the handcuffed man coming back to our neighborhood looking for me. I decided he wasn't as innocent as he looked. He probably killed children and hid them in the gulch. I was sure I was next.

Everyone on the bus was talking about the murder that happened behind my house. I secretly was amazed how I started a rumor and everyone was talking about it. Kids I didn't know came up to me and asked me questions about the murderer. As the day went by, my stories got more and more intricate. I think I had a real knack for telling a story. The problem was, the more I told a lie, the more I started to believe it and it became my history.

After school, Len and the two Tim's came and got me to go into the gulch to look for the dead body. "I think it is a kid," I said.

"I think it is two kids," Len said. We slid down the same steep bank that the police had brought the prisoner up. There were skid marks from where their shoes slid in the dirt. I was terrified but didn't say anything. Being down in it, it was darker and the bushes were thicker than I imagined. What if there was another murderer down here. My nerves were on edge.

Suddenly Timmy put a small gardener snake in my face. I let out a blood curdling scream that would have echoed up and out of the gulch if the thick vegetation hadn't absorbed most of the sound. Tim began to laugh hysterically and I became infuriated. "Are you afraid of snakes?" he said in a singsong, high-pitched voice as he swung the snake back and forth in front of my face.

I reached out and he jumped back. "Let me see it," I said, even though I wanted nothing to do with the disgusting, slimy reptile, but he wasn't going to get to me. I continue to move towards him, trying to grab the snake, and he kept moving away until he finally gave up and threw it deep into the bush. I concentrated hard not to show the relief on my face.

There were lots of benefits to living in government housing—free lunch, summer camp and lots of classes. The lunches at school were amazing and I ate almost everything they gave me. The only thing I didn't really like was the chili, but I would make it work by pouring some of my milk in it so it wasn't too spicy.

Summer camp was really a day camp at Horseshoe Lake. My mom and all my sisters went to the lake all day. They taught us how to boil thistles so you could eat them. We learned what kind of berries we could eat and which ones were poisonous. We already knew that huckleberries and salal berries were okay. They also showed us how to mix our powdered milk with chocolate to make chocolate milk. We made pancakes with the brown bag mix when we got our welfare food.

Unless we had to babysit the little kids, Teresa and I would go to the Community Center. We took ballet, tap and tumbling classes.

We also learned how to sew with a modern sewing machine, where all you had to do was plug it in and step on a pedal. It was a lot more complicated to thread than Beverly's old fashioned machine, but I learned pretty fast. My first project was making an apron, which I gave my mom, but we weren't really the apron kind of people.

The next project was real clothes. We went to the fabric store and picked out a Simplicity pattern with some funky wide leg pants and a matching top that you pull over your head and tie with a homemade belt. The fabric we picked out was black and gold polyester. The instructor barely had to help us. The worst part was pinning the pattern pieces to the fabric inside out and cutting the edges, careful not to cut off the diamonds because that is how you would line up the pieces before you sew. I just wanted to get to the sewing part.

The best part of being poor was the government food. Once a week, my parents would bring home boxes of food all in brown wrappings. Bread just had the word "Bread" on the packaging, rice said "Rice," beans said "Beans," and peanut butter said "Peanut Butter." Once in a while they bought real name brand cereal like Cheerios or Frosted Flakes, but the powdered milk ruined the taste. Still, it was better than eating the powdered eggs.

Near the end of the week all we had left was the butter, eggs and tortillas. If we were really hungry, we would put butter and sugar on a tortilla as a snack and, if we were really lucky, we would have some cheese left from the huge block of cheddar cheese and we could make quesadillas. The only problem with the cheese usually was that it would get hard and oily in the refrigerator because we didn't have plastic wrap or foil to cover it.

Food wasn't the only issue. Other items we needed we often ran out of, including toilet paper. My mom would say, "just use a washcloth," but there were only so many washcloths and we had to share. This was the only time I wished we still lived in the cabin where there were plenty of soft leaves.

Chapter 9

Dad was not home very much when we lived in the cabin because he was selling wood, but now he was gone for days at a time. He was part of a two-man traveling sales team selling custom signs focusing on small businesses but mostly the "mom and pops."

The signs were white plastic bubbles that lighted up from the inside, and the business name appeared in bright colors on both sides. Anytime I saw one of these signs, I wondered if my dad had sold it to them. I like to think he had. In some poorer neighborhoods in Tacoma, you can still see a few of these promoting "Sewing Machine Repair" or "Beer"—except they had lost the vibrant color and are faded and cracked.

The next evolution of this was a sign that would say whatever you wanted. You would program a message and red letters would move across a long black screen advertising whatever you wanted. Next, it would flash the time and date and then roll the message across once again. This sign was going to change our lives. Everyone was going to want one.

With dad gone so much we spent a lot of time at home since we didn't have another car and my mom didn't really drive. One time when dad left the car, she loaded us all up and we went to her school downtown. She ended up going down a one-way street almost getting us in an accident and we were stopped by a cop because of the amount of black smoke coming from our exhaust. I think the cop felt sorry for us and let us go. "Just get it fixed," he said, shaking his head as he walked back to his own car, looking at us through our dirty windows. We took the bus from then on.

Mom seemed to really like beauty school, even though she told us she had a hard time in school and barely made it to graduation. She studied all the time. We would help her memorize terms and she would practice techniques on us. Even her own hair changed. Her long red hair was cut into a short permed fashionable afro style with a blonde frame and dark hair in the back. She looked like she just walked out of a fashion magazine.

"You look ridiculous," my dad said when he saw her. She had dressed up in a short mini skirt and go-go boots to surprise him. She started to cry and one of her false eyelashes fell off when she put her hands over her face. My dad felt bad and he put his arms around her.

"Cherri, go get your mom a glass of water," he told me, since I was standing there watching for his reaction. I knew my mom was excited to surprise him. I thought her hair was very fashionable. It reminded me of a lion's mane. "I told you not to cut your hair unless you check with me," I heard him say when I was in the kitchen.

"It's her hair," I said as I handed my mom the water. They both looked at me, shocked. My mom now really did look ridiculous with one set of eyelashes gone and the other fluttering up and down, black makeup in lines down her face.

"This is none of your business," my dad said. "Go play in your room." This would not be the last time I would have words with my father. My mother, apparently, couldn't stand up for herself, so I had to stand up for her.

"I will never let anyone boss me around when I get older," I said as I left them.

My dad must have felt bad because, about a half hour later, they headed out the door to get some dinner. My mom was her happy self with her face back.

"Watch the girls, we will be back in a while. Daddy is taking me to Chinese," she said to Teresa and me.

"There is no food here," I said

"There's food. You can figure it out."

They left, and Teresa and I went to the kitchen, looking at what we could make the girls for dinner. We cut up some bologna and tore up tortillas into small pieces and fried it all up in a cast iron pan. When it was cooked, we added the few eggs we had combined with some powdered eggs so there would be enough. The girls loved it.

Babysitting was always a challenge because Josette and Angie always made messes and we would get in trouble if our parents came home to a messy house. If we were mean to them they would tell on us and we would get in trouble for that too.

The hall closet became the perfect solution. We put folded up blankets on the floor and strung an electrical cord to plug in a lamp so they would have light. We put a couple toys in there and some playing cards to keep them busy.

"You guys get to be in a cave," I told them.

"I'm not getting in there," Lisa said. Sometimes Lisa was a big girl and sometimes a little girl, depending on the activity. She often complained that she was never included in either group, but we ignored her.

The two youngest were excited to get into the cave and happily squeezed in next to the vacuum cleaner. They actually stayed in there until it was bedtime. The only things they ruined were the playing cards. They ripped off the top of each one, pretending the card was a package of Kool-Aid which they opened. I collected all the pieces and put the cards and the tops of the cards in the garbage, reaching far under the egg carton and other garbage so my mom wouldn't see the damage. We put the lamp back on the night table in our parent's room and went to bed.

I'm not sure what time our parents got home, but they were loud and woke us up. I couldn't tell if they were fighting or happy and I didn't want to know. I would pretend to be asleep if they even bothered to check on us. Angie started crying and got into bed with Teresa. Teresa slept so soundly, sometimes I would check her breath to make sure she wasn't dead. I was lucky nobody wanted to get in bed with me. They said I kicked and hit when I was asleep. You didn't want to sleep with Lisa or have her in your bed because she was a rocker. She would curl up and rock back and forth until she fell asleep. You could always tell when she was doing it because her bed squeaked.

The next day, we were happy to see there were Chinese leftovers for breakfast. My mom would combine and fry up the white rice, fried rice and whatever chow mien was left in the bottom of the boxes. Any leftover fried prawns were coveted—she kept them for herself and ate them cold. Occasionally, we could have a bite.

1915: Clara (Age 28)

Clara was excited about the séance. She hoped she would be able to communicate with her mother. She wanted to ask her if baby Della was with her.

Clara was disappointed when Walter staggered in the door. He glared over at his three small daughters and headed to the kitchen. She couldn't leave the girls with him in his state.

"Where is my dinner?" His words were slurred. He stumbled while pulling out a chair and fell into it. Clara turned and put a glass of water in front of him. His black eyes narrowed and he backhanded the glass from the table where it hit the wall with a loud crash. Three-year-old Helen started to cry, but seven-year-old Dorris and five-year-old Lena quickly hushed their younger sister, fearing their father's wrath.

"God damn it woman, I want my dinner," he yelled, putting emphasis on "damn".

"It's almost ready." Clara opened the oven and looked in, but there wasn't much there. Walter hadn't worked in a while and there was no money. The few potatoes she had were from her own garden. Walter pulled a flask from his inside pocket and took a swig. He seemed a little more relaxed. Clara was sweeping the broken shards of glass from the floor as he watched her.

In a sudden movement, he grabbed her arm and pulled her towards him. With both hands, he grabbed her shirt and pulled it apart, buttons flying.

"What's this?" he yelled, pushing his fist to her stomach.

Clara started to shake. "I'm pregnant."

"Pregnant," he screamed and pushed her across the room. "You fucking whore!"

"It's your baby," she said softly.

"Liar!" Walter had the mumps the year before and the doctor told him that one of the effects was that he was now sterile. He grabbed her by the hair and dragged her out of the kitchen and into the living room where the three girls sat hanging on to each other in terror.

"See this, girls?" Clara was on the floor, tears running down her face. Walter had his foot on her back. "This is what a no good ungrateful cheating lying whore looks like." He pulled his foot back and kicked her in the side. The girls screamed but covered their mouths. Walter picked up his wife by the hair, opened the front door and pushed her with his foot propelling her a few feet where she hit the ground.

Clara laid on the ground for a few minutes getting her breath back. She got up slowly. There was a sharp pain in her chest, and she was pretty sure Walter had broken her ribs. She walked slowly, stopping every few feet to get her breath. She held her hands across her belly, praying the baby growing inside her was okay. She finally reached the neighbors front door, where she collapsed.

The next thing she knew, she was in a hospital, not sure how long she had been there.

"How are you feeling, dear?" asked an older nurse standing at the foot of the bed. Clara tried to sit up but the pain in her chest was too strong. "We have sent word to your husband," she said.

"No!" Clara started to cry but choked at the pain throughout her body. "Where are my children?"

"I'm not sure, dear," she said.

Walter didn't show up at the hospital and Clara was released a week later to her brother, who took her with him to Portland. Florence Evelyn was born July 15, 1915, and was given up for adoption the next day.

V

1974: Charisse (Age 11)

Chapter 10

Eventually, Mom grew her hair out and dyed it back to her normal Lucille Ball red.

Dad continued to be on the road, where he would make his fortune. "You can never get ahead working for someone else," he said.

My mom always did whatever my dad said. He acted like her boss. She had no access to money. He wrote all the checks for bills and gave her a little bit of money for certain things. We couldn't go grocery shopping without him, and he was the one who picked out what we bought. He told her when to drink water and she would do it.

But because he was gone so much, Mom started to have her own life with friends from beauty school. Sometimes we would go with her on the bus to keep her company, but we couldn't hang out at the shop so we would wander around downtown. It wasn't a long ride downtown but it was something to do. Her classes were about two hours long, so we could walk around downtown or ride the bus back home. If the little girls stayed with Aunt Wilma, we would walk down Broadway, looking into the stores and watching homeless people.

The main Tacoma public library was not too far from the beauty school, so it was a great place to hang out. It was cool in the summer and warm in the winter. It was so big, the librarians hardly noticed you were there and didn't pay attention to what you checked out. At the library close to our house, it was harder to get a book that wasn't age appropriate. The librarian was an old lady who carefully looked over every book I put on the counter. She would only let me check out two at a time, and she would pick the two. One time she even made me pick out different books than I had already picked.

Since the library downtown didn't pay attention and let me check out whatever I wanted, I chose a paperback, "Looking for Mr. Goodbar," by Judith Rossner. When I checked it out, I really thought it had something to do with candy bars.

My mother never noticed or questioned what I was reading. It was one of those books that the local librarian wouldn't have let me check out. The main character was Theresa Dunn, a young woman living a double life. She was an innocent teacher who went to singles bars at night. She took someone home from the bar and he killed her. It was not appropriate for a fifth grader, but I couldn't put it down.

Mom was at school and Teresa and I were watching the girls. Lisa was being a pain and was making me mad. We were in the middle of creating a new recipe, like we often did when we were left by ourselves. We took out whatever was available in the refrigerator or cupboards and mixed it together. Lisa was our usual guinea pig.
"I'm going to tell on you." It was like the fourth time she said it.
"Go ahead," I said. "You will be sorry."
"You are the one who is going to be sorry," she said.
"Here, drink this." I handed her a glass of lemonade we had mixed some apple juice into. For some reason, she drank it.
"How is it?"
"It tastes weird."
"It's because I peed in it." I started to laugh and she started to cry. Sometimes I felt bad if I made my sisters cry, but not today. I tried to get Teresa to actually pee in it, before we gave it to Lisa but she wouldn't.
"Everybody is so mean to me," Lisa cried. "I hate living here. I am going to run away."
Now that was a great idea. Teresa and I helped her pack a pillowcase with clothes. We gave her some raisins and half a package of saltine crackers. We tied her pillowcase at the end and said our good byes. Josette and Angelique stood by in shock. They didn't want her to go. We all walked to the end of the sidewalk and watched her walk out of view. We went back in the house, relieved that she was gone. It wasn't long before she came back. I was sort of glad, because my mom and dad would probably have been mad that we let her run away.

Mom continued studying and practicing her beauty techniques. Most of the practice was on us five girls. She didn't want to cut my long blonde hair but would use thinning shears on me. She fought with me almost every day trying to get a brush through my long, thick hair. I consistently had knots of hair underneath that she pulled on and sometimes had to cut out.

I would fuss and cry. "It hurts," I would complain.

"It hurts to be beautiful," was her standard answer to any of us if we yelled or cried when she practiced on us.

Mom passed both her written test and practical test and was now a licensed cosmetologist. She sent her applications to a few places. One was right down the street from where she went to school. My dad took her to the interview, but he didn't wait in the car. He decided to go into the interview with her. He took over and barely let my mom speak. She did get the job, but her new boss said, "Bernice, never take your husband on an interview again."

The job didn't last long. Dad got a Union job and was going to make "good money" so my mom could stay home and take care of her five kids.

VI

1975 Charisse (Age 12)

Chapter 11

Living on Fawcett Street was the turning point for us. We felt like we finally made it into the middle class. We lived in a five-bedroom, two-story house on a corner lot with a big basement, in a real neighborhood, because my dad had a real job at West Coast Grocery, which came along with all the benefits of the Teamsters Union.

One of the first things we did was go to the dentist. Besides multiple fillings and pulling teeth, we all eventually got braces, including my mom, who had always been embarrassed by her overbite. We went to the doctor for checkups and I finally got fit for the special shoes I needed to correct my duck feet.

We were able to take dance lessons and play instruments. Teresa and I took private flute lessons by a young woman in North Tacoma.

It was America's 200th birthday, so we had lots of activities in school that year for the bicentennial. Mr. Laws was my 6th grade teacher. At first, I was nervous about having a male teacher, but he was the best teacher I ever had. My best friends were Lulu and Janet. I never really had best friends before, so sometimes I didn't know how to act. Most of the kids in my school had known each other since they were in Kindergarten. I had a crush on Richard Thayer, a cute blonde-haired boy who was constantly getting in trouble.

There was going to be a big parade for the bicentennial celebration, and our class was going to perform a square dance in the parade. My partner was Richard. I couldn't believe my luck. I was in Love. But it turned out that Richard was so mean I could hardly stand being his partner.

"You know what you are?" he asked me.

"What?"

"A carpenter's dream…flat as a board." He laughed hysterically. My face turned red but I didn't start crying. He was so cruel to me.

I never really thought about what I wore or how I looked. The only time I had tried to dress older, I wore my mother's orange velvet hot pants and matching top, completing the outfit with panty hose and go-go boots. I walked into the school so confident that even the boy that dressed up like the Fonz everyday would notice me. The problem was that everybody noticed me. "Nice legs," some of the boys started chanting. I was so devastated, I went into the bathroom and took off the panty hose.

I endured other humiliation by my elementary school peers. My mother was oblivious to my pointy breasts, which had made their appearance and were even more pronounced when I wore tight turtle neck sweaters, which were my favorite. It was again the boys at school taunting me with "You're a carpenter's dream…Flat as a board." Or "You're a pirate's dream…Sunkin' Chest." Their taunts didn't even make sense since I was as well-endowed as most of the girls in my class. My dad was the one who took me to the store to get my first bra. I could tell the lady at the store felt sorry for me because she loaded me up with several options and sent me to the dressing room. I only knew how to fasten them by watching my mother put hers on. I was past the need for a training bra and left the store with a women's size A.

I was surprised when I got a note from Greg, another boy from our class. He was shorter than me and had bright blue eyes, auburn red hair and freckles all over his face and arms. He even had freckles on his hands, but he had a nice smile. The note read:

Will you be my girlfriend?
_____Yes
_____No
_____Maybe
Check one

I flushed with embarrassment. I never had a boyfriend. I panicked when he walked by, and stuck my tongue out at him. His face turned red and he sat back at his desk, defeated. Richard was in the back of the room making chicken noises while other boys laughed. I didn't turn around in case they were making fun of me.

But the love of my life was Richard Thayer, my biggest tormentor in elementary school. He would sit behind me in class and snap my bra. I would never tell on him. I was too in "love."

At recess, I showed Lulu and Janet the note from Greg. Lulu said I should say yes.

"He is cute," she said.

"He is short," I said.

"Everyone except Dawn and Richard is shorter than you," Lulu said. She was right. I was already 5'7" at 12 years old. Richard was the same height as me, and Dawn was so tall she looked like an adult. She was big and walked around with her head down. The boys made fun of her all the time. They called her the "jolly green giant" and asked her how the weather was up there.

Lulu's boyfriend was the coolest boy in 6th grade. He wore a black leather jacket and slicked his hair back like Fonzie on the show Happy Days. Happy Days was our favorite show and we ran home after school not to miss it.

"I would say no," Janet said.

I marked _X___ Maybe, and Lulu delivered the note back to him.

He asked me again a few days later when he came over to my house with Jeff, who was Teresa's age, and Todd, Greg's best friend, who was also in my class. He took me to the side of the house. "Do you want to be my girlfriend now?"

"Sure. I guess," I said nervously, moving my hair out of my face by tucking it behind my ears.

"We have to kiss to make it real," he said. The only people I ever kissed were my grandparents and it was disgusting. I knew this was different and I couldn't help myself.

"Okay." Panic welled up inside me. I didn't really know how to kiss and he was so much shorter than me it would be awkward. I took him to the back porch and had him stand on the second step so we would be closer in height. Our lips met in the middle. His lips were soft and sweet. He had a big wad of Bubble Yum in his mouth and it filled my nose like sweet relief.

When he tried to stick his tongue in my mouth, I pulled back with embarrassment. I had a mouth full of braces and didn't know how to reciprocate. What if my braces cut his tongue?

We broke up a few weeks later when I found out Greg was dating another girl in our class. It was quite the scandal among us girls in the sixth grade, but I recovered fast.

There were other boys in the neighborhood, Jeff Dillinger, Todd Fleming, and Jimmy Lean, and we all hung around in a group. Jimmy was a handsome blonde-haired, blue-eyed boy that feathered his hair like Andy Gibb. He lived just a few blocks away and hung out with Jeff Dillinger. Both these boys had cool dispositions that made them more attractive. They rode their bikes by our house, stopping to chat for a few minutes, and then took off to go do boy things.

"Are you going skating?" Jimmy asked me. He sat on his modified bike that looked too small for him, but he could do cool tricks on it.

"Probably," I said, but I had no idea what he was talking about. I had never been skating in my life, but I would figure it out.

"Cool. See you there."

"Cool," I said. I walked towards Lulu's house. She lived just a few blocks away. I was crossing 45th street when a car slowed and stopped in front of me. A bald white man with a large gap in between his front teeth rolled down the window.

"Hey beautiful. Do you know where Mulligan Street is?" He smiled too big and held up a map.

"I've never heard of that street," I said.

"It's right here on the map," he said, pointing to the map. I took a step closer but he lowered it further into his lap. "I think we are right here." He pointed down. I walked right up to the window and looked in. It took a minute for me to register what I was looking at as I focused on his hand, which was moving up and down on his bare cock. It looked like a giant one-eyed slug looking up at me. I stepped back and focused back into the man's face where the smile was still there, frozen like a clown smile, but it wasn't a smile, it was satisfaction. Finally, the panic welled up and took over when he reached for the door handle, and I ran.

The car was between my house and me, so I turned and ran the other way, cutting across yards. I didn't look back, afraid he was chasing me. When I reached the alley behind Lulu's house, I ducked between two garbage cans to get my breath. He couldn't have chased me on foot, because I don't think he was wearing pants, but I stayed for a few minutes listening for a car. When I didn't hear anything, I got up and went through the back gate and knocked on Lulu's door.

Lulu was home alone, so when I told her what happened, we went through the house closing the drapes and peering out every time we heard a car go by to see if he was looking for me. I didn't want to go home. I didn't want to call my mom and tell her because she might freak out and I knew my dad wasn't home anyway, so we decided to call Jimmy and Jeff. We told them about the creep, so when they showed up at Lulu's house, Jeff was carrying a baseball bat and Jimmy had his nunchucks. We hung out at Lulu's for a while before the boys walked me home, Jimmy confidently swinging his nunchucks in different configurations. I was impressed.

I was surprised when Jimmy kissed me at my front door. This would be the first kiss of many more make out sessions. Whenever my parents went out, Jimmy would come over and we would make out in the back yard. When my parents came home, he would jump over the back fence and I would go in the back door.

VII

1976: Charisse (Age 13)

Chapter 12

Teresa, Lisa and I walked down to Lively Market down on Pacific to get mom a cup of coffee and some penny candy. The store was only four blocks away, and we made the trip at least once a day for coffee, milk or toilet paper. Dad would leave change on his dresser and I would sift through it, taking a quarter, a nickel and a few pennies, nothing he would notice. I figured he owed me for all the times he said he was going to pay us allowance and never did or the few times we did get allowance and my mom had to borrow it back to buy milk and never paid me back.

"Hey Oreo Cookie," John called out from across the street. He was surrounded by his little gang of hooligans, who all laughed. It looked like they were doing surgery on a skateboard. I just flipped them off.

"I'm going to tell." Lisa was always going to tell on me. She was cute but annoying.

"What are you going to tell?" I said, rolling my eyes. "I didn't do anything."

"That you flipped the bird," she said confidently.

"Go ahead. I will remember that when we are in the store. How much money do you have?"

"None."

"Well you can wait outside then, or go home."

Lisa's defiant face turned soft as she realized her mistake. "Okay, I won't tell."

"You can't always tell the parents everything," I told her. "Do you think they tell you everything? What good would it do if I was on restriction?"

"Why did they call you an Oreo Cookie?"

"Because you and Teresa are brown and I am white. Get it?"

Teresa didn't say anything. Teresa never told on me no matter how bad the offense. I wasn't a rule follower. I did whatever I wanted unless my dad was home. If my mom told me "no" for anything, I would follow her around the house, crying, begging and torturing her until she would explode and scream as loud as she could, "Just do it then!"

I would happily walk out the door to go to my friends, ride to the mall, or whatever. Teresa would feel bad. "We shouldn't go."

"I did not just spend all that time and energy for nothing. I am going!" Sometimes she would stay but most of the time she went with me, and my mother was back to normal when we got back home.

The store was a mom and pop type of market where everyone who worked there knew us. It had a little bit of everything. Today, right inside the door, was a huge display of Billy Beer that we had to walk around to get to the candy isle. There was a full isle with candy on both sides. The section of penny candy was where we spent most of our money. I had just over a dollar in change plus the fifty-five cents my mom gave us for her cup of coffee. It took us at least a half hour to pick out 50 pieces, 10 pieces each. We would split it up with the little girls at home later. We also bought some pop rocks and a candy bar to share on our way home.

We took turns holding the large hot coffee on our way up the hill. Still a few blocks away, we could see a giant 18-wheel truck parked at the side of the house. It took up all the space from the alley to the front of the house.

As soon as we walked in the house, you could smell the strong scent of aftershave followed by a deep voice coming from the kitchen. It was Grandpa White sitting at the kitchen table with mom. Angelique and Josette each sat on one of his legs.

I smiled and put the coffee on the table so I could put my arms around his neck. I am not sure why I was so happy to see Grandpa but I could almost feel tears welling up. The girls spotted the small brown bag bulging with candy and got down and went over to Teresa. My mom went to the cupboard and pulled out two mugs. She poured the black coffee evenly into the mugs and handed one to grandpa.

"Is that your truck?" I asked grandpa.

"Yep," Grandpa said with a big smile. "I'm driving a long hauler now." As he said this I noticed the difference in my mom's dad. He used to be a redneck painting contractor with a buzz cut, now his red hair was combed back and was almost touching his shoulders. He was wearing a light blue t-shirt, worn blue jeans and an Indian-beaded necklace around his neck. He looked like a hippy but with a wrinkly face.

"Do you want to go with Grandpa and stay with Punky for a few weeks?" my mom asked. I looked at Grandpa and he was smiling and nodding his head.

"Now?" I excitingly looked between them. "In the truck?" They both nodded their heads up and down together. I ran to my room and threw my clothes into a garbage sack.

It took almost 5 hours to get to Grandpa's house in Eugene. I rode in the sleeper behind the cab area, peeking my head out to talk to Grandpa. The truck was empty after he had made a delivery to Seattle. He usually tried to fill the truck for the ride home, but there wasn't anything available and he wanted to take a few days off anyway. I fell asleep for part of the time and we talked for part of the time, and I listened to him talk on the CB to other drivers. I only understood half of what they talked about.

Last time I had seen Punky was a few years ago when we were just little girls and we sat together at the kitchen table where she showed me how to stay in the lines easier when we were coloring. It must have been around Christmas time because I remember Grandma White had crocheted us each slippers and matching scarfs in different colors. Mine were green.

Now we were young teenagers, things were different between us. She wore makeup and high waisted jeans that flared out wide at the bottom. I still felt like a little girl. I kept my mouth shut and followed her around. It was the opposite of how I was at home, when my sisters followed me around. The house was so much quieter than it had been before. It was almost like she was an only child. Her two sisters, Vicki and Terry, were both married and had small children, and her brother, Rick, who still lived at home, was busy with sports and school. He was never home. He was about to graduate and go off to join the military.

"Do you get high?" she asked me. I knew what pot was because I went across the alley to Cody's house. Everyone called it the hippy house because there were a lot of young people living in one house and they all smoked pot. I had a small crush on Cody, but he always called me "little sister." One time he drew a peace sign on my favorite pair of jeans. I didn't wash them for weeks, afraid the ink would wash out. My mom finally got to them and the peace sign almost faded out, I had to trace it with a pen so it wouldn't disappear. I was going to save those jeans forever.

"No," I said. "Do you?"

"Of course, I do," she said. "Do you want to?"

"I guess." I was nervous but excited. I was only 13 and a half but felt a lot older.

Punky had thin brown hair that hung a little past her shoulders. She had big brown eyes and a big wide smile. I studied her face, looking for similarities to my mom since she was her half-sister, but since she was only six months older than me it was hard to see a resemblance. The whole family thing was confusing.

Punky led me up to the attic, which had been turned into a bedroom with a couch and a dresser. Punky opened the dresser and pulled out a plastic bag full of marijuana. She pulled an empty bag out of her pocket and carefully transferred some from one bag to the other.

"Don't tell my mom or dad," she said. "My mom doesn't know my dad smokes pot." She rolled her bag and stuck it into her pocket.

Grandma was still exactly as I remembered. She was tall and thin with dark black hair carefully teased and sprayed in place. When she smiled, huge dimples appeared on both cheeks. She was in the kitchen wearing a yellow apron with ruffles on both sides and a big pocket in front. She reminded me of a "Leave It to Beaver" kind of mom, except older with dark hair. Since Grandpa changed into more of a hippy, they didn't match as much.

"Come give Grandma Green a big hug." She had an oversized fork in her hand and I put my arms around her and hugged her tight. Last time I was here, my arms went around her waist. I was as tall as she was now. I don't remember when I had started calling her "Grandma Green"—apparently, when I was young I decided she was my favorite grandma, so instead of calling her Grandma White I started calling her Grandma Green because green was my favorite color.

"I'm making roast for dinner," she said.

"Yummmm, my favorite," I said.

"I remember." She winked at me and Punky rolled her eyes.

"Let's go," Punky said roughly, pushing the back-screen door open. I caught it half way before it slammed in my face as I followed her out.

We walked across the street to a single-story house. The house looked worn out and tired, like it had been painted white but now was more grey from dirt and sun exposure. The front door was wide open and we walked right in like we lived there. The house was small and crowded with furniture. Punky headed straight for the kitchen with me following close behind.

"Hey Rila," she said to a girl who looked about our age but with long black hair that was almost down to her knees. She stood at the stove frying a flat piece of dough. An old lady, wearing a colorful scarf over her head and tied under her chin, sat at the kitchen table so still I thought she might be a statue. I visibly jumped when she moved to take a drink from her small, delicate tea cup.

"Baba, want some bread?" Rila put a piece fresh from the oil onto a napkin and set it in front of her grandmother without waiting for an answer. She also put another piece on another napkin and handed it to Punky. She took it, sat at the table and instantly took a careful bite.

"Would you like to try Gypsy bread?" Rila asked me as I sat next to Punky and directly across from the grandmother. I accepted the fried bread and was surprised at how delicious it was.

"Tea?" the grandmother asked me as she reached across the table for a cup.

"No, thank you," I said.

"I'll read your leaves," she said as she poured a cup only about a fourth full.

"It's rude to say no," Punky said. Rila sat in the fourth chair.

"She is really good at it," Rila said, chewing on her piece of bread.

She had me swish the tea around, take a small drink and repeat the process several times until there was less than a teaspoon of tea at the bottom. She took the cup from my hands and poured the remaining drops into the saucer. She then turned it upside down and closed her eyes, keeping both hands on the bottom.

She moved her hands. "Please turn it over," she said quietly. The other two girls watched like they had seen this process a thousand times. I turned it over and placed it into her outstretched hand. She looked into where the small particles of tea had stuck together in different parts of the cup.

"Bakalo," she said, smiling. "You are a lucky girl in your life but you will face complications now and again. Here is a 'crown' which represents a wish coming true in the near future." She turned the cup a quarter turn and pointed to another glob of tea remnant's. "This looks like a 'buckle', which means some disappointments ahead." She turned the cup again. I watched her carefully. Her face had no expression, she looked like a painting. "There is a 'fish', good fortune in health, wealth and happiness, but there are tears." She pointed to a few drops of tea that had stayed in the cup even after we had turned it over. "Complicated." It was the last thing she said before she took the last bite of her bread and another sip of the tea that sat in front of her. Then she froze into the same position she was sitting in when we first walked into the kitchen. It was like she was a robot that was turned on for a few minutes and was now turned back off. A shiver went down my spine.

Punky broke the spell when she asked Rila, "We are going to the Pay and Save, do you want to go?"

Rila turned off the stove and grabbed her bag. Punky and Rila became friends the first day Rila moved in, a few months before the end of the school year. The three of us got on a city bus a block away from the house. We sat in the very back seat. Rila told me she was home schooled and was getting married in September after she turned 16. She had only met her husband one time when they were young children but he was from a good family. I wasn't sure if she was telling me the truth or fooling around. We got off the bus one block away from the Pay & Save so the girls could have a smoke. It was surprising watching Punky smoke.

"Want one?" Punky stuck the pack in my direction.

"No thanks," I said. They finished up and we walked into the store and down several isles of makeup and costume jewelry. I watched the girls pick up items and return them to the shelves.

"What are you going to get?" Punky asked me.

"I don't have any money," I said. She grabbed a pair of earrings and held them up to the light, examining them, and with her other hand reached out and took another pair and slipped it into her pocket.

"That's how you do it. You can drop one and when you pick it up slip the other hand into your pocket. It's easy," she said. I had never shoplifted before but had thought about it many times at Lively Market, where it would have been so easy to slip some gum into my pocket when the cashier wasn't looking.

I looked through the earrings for one I wanted. It was a pair of black and silver teardrops that I finally palmed and carried around—my heart beating so hard I could barely breathe. Finally, I put them into the front pocket of my tan corduroy pants. I was glad they were loose fitting because I wasn't smooth and I was sure I was going to get caught.

Now all I wanted to do was get out of there. I stood near the door waiting for the other girls, occasionally moving into the trigger that opened the door and rang the bell, causing more attention to myself than necessary. I awkwardly smiled at the other people coming in and out of the store until finally the girls confidently walked out and I followed. They again pulled out cigarettes and with steady hands lit them and casually walked back to the same bus stop.

When we reached the bus stop close to the house, Punky reached up and pulled the bell wire that signaled the driver to stop, but instead of going home, the girls headed down the sidewalk in the opposite direction. We climbed over a wooden four-foot fence and into a garage where there were four other teenagers, three guys and a girl, sitting on old couches and on the floor. In the center of the group there was a giant bong that one of the guys sucked hard at. I watched the smoke travel up the glass tube where he breathed it in. He let go and the smoke cleared as he took his head back, holding it in for a few seconds before he smoothly blew a long stream of smoke up over our heads.

Punky sat on the worn couch that leaned to one side like a foot was missing. She patted the space next to her, motioning me to sit. Rila sat on the floor on a piece of torn carpet, facing us. There were multiple carpet remnants pieced together to make a defined space where it appeared these kids hung out.

Rila dumped her big bag onto the floor. Makeup, several tubes of lip gloss, gum, rings and earrings all spilled out in front of her. I could not imagine how she got away with all the stuff without being caught. I hadn't seen her take one thing, but I wasn't really paying attention.

Punky pulled her pot out of her pocket and grabbed a tray from the wooden box they were using as a table. I watched her pick through the pot, taking out seeds and stems and putting them to one side. She took a pack of white papers and spread the bits that were now free of the seeds and stems. She rolled it into a perfect joint. She lit it and took a big puff and handed it to her left, where the boy with feathered blond hair also took a big toke. The joint went around the room until it came to me. It was pretty small, and before I took it from Rila, Punky took the clip from her hair and attached it to the end with a pinch. I held the clip that had two long feathers hanging from it. I sucked the joint but nothing happened. Punky showed me how to suck in without actually touching it. I did it how she showed me and sucked plenty of smoke. It burned as I felt it travel down my throat and into my lungs where I held it as long as I could. When I blew it out, I started to cough uncontrollably. Everyone started to laugh and I was embarrassed.

After the next few rounds, I was a master at smoking pot and I was very high. I couldn't stop laughing and fell over the fence when I tried to jump across. It didn't even hurt.

When I got home two weeks later, I was a different girl. I had two joints in a black plastic film container and was wearing my stolen earrings and a bad ass attitude.

1926: Helen Warren (age 14)

Helen was looking forward to seeing her mother again. Dorris had turned 18 so the state had given her custody of her two younger sisters, Lena and Helen, 16 and 14, who were living at a Catholic run orphanage since they were taken from their father years before. Helen remembered the day the people from the state came to her home. Her father had been gone for a few days and they had no food, but when the woman tried to convince her to get in the car, she sat down defiantly, insisting "My daddy said I don't go with strangers." The woman had no patience and simply picked her up and threw her in next to her sisters.

Lena and Helen had been kept together at the orphanage until a family took them in. The arrangement didn't last long. The father of the house had tried to molest them and they decided to get out. The girls threw fits and wet their beds, so they were finally returned to the orphanage.

Clara had married Charlie, a good-natured house painter, and they had two baby girls, Edith, 6, and Marion barely a year. Charlie's previous wife died and left him two sons who also lived at the house. The house was nearly full and included Charlie's cantankerous father, but Clara wanted the girls to live with her so they made room.

Lena and Helen took on most of the child care duties of their two little sisters while their mother worked as a housekeeper for other people. They fit into their new family and enjoyed hanging out with the two boys, Julius and Alvin.

At fourteen, Helen couldn't help falling in love with her step-brother, Alvin, who was funny as well as handsome. The relationship was, of course, forbidden, but they secretly confessed their love for each other. It wasn't long before Helen was pregnant, so they had no choice but to approach their parents.

"We would like to get married," Alvin said to his father and step-mother.

Clara and Charlie looked at each other and then at the two children standing in front of them.

"Absolutely not!" Clara stood up in front of her daughter. "She is fourteen." She turned to Alvin.

"What were you thinking?" Charlie asked his son.

"This situation cannot leave this room," Clara said, pointing at the two. "You will tell no one. Do you understand?"

Tears rolled down Helen's face. "But I love him."

"You are too young to love anyone."

"You," she pointed to Alvin, "you need to get out of town. I don't care where you go, but you go." Charlie nodded. He would miss his boy, but the scandal would be too much.

Both Alvin and Julius were packed up and put on a train to California where they would work on a grain farm.

Helen was confined to the house until May 23, 1927 when she gave birth to Nelda Mae in the front bedroom of their home in Seattle. The birth certificate lists Charlie Vesper Brashears as the father and Clara Nelly Brashears as the mother. Nelda was never told her mother was actually Helen and her father Alvin.

VIII

1977: Charisse (Age 14)

Chapter 13

I wasn't thrilled about camping but it was hot out and I loved swimming at the lake so when my parents brought us to Black Lake, I didn't mind. We put up tents and built a circle of rocks for the camp fire. We brought firewood and an ice chest with some soda and sandwiches. We spent the weekend as a family. Teresa and I decided it was a good idea to try to swim across the lake. Once we got there, we were too tired to swim back, but had no choice, so we did it but had to rest by floating on our backs. About half way, I started to panic. I was tired and I knew I couldn't stop so I kept going.

Sunday night, my dad and mom packed up the girls and headed home, leaving Teresa and me at the campsite. We spent the next few days swimming and laying out on our towels in the sun. The parents came back Thursday after work and picked us up so we could get clean clothes and take showers.

I asked my dad if the boys could come with us camping, and to my surprise he said yes. I called Jimmy and Jeff and they came over with sleeping bags. We all piled up in the back of the truck and went camping. We set up a second tent where the boys would sleep.

We spent the next few days swimming and walking around the lake. I was showing off and accidently hit my head on the trailer so hard I had a goose sized egg on my forehead. I couldn't cry in front of the boys so I suffered in silence. There was a pay phone about half a mile away but I figured, even if I did call my mom, she wouldn't have a way to come get me.

When we came home, Shelly and Sheila came over with their new sister. I was in the basement playing ping pong with Teresa and Lisa. We took turns or played doubles. Shelly and Sheila lived down the block on the same side in a big white house with blue trim, opposite of our blue house with white trim. Shelly was Lisa's age and Sheila was Josette's age. Jenni was the girls' step-sister, who recently came to live with them.

"Are you adopted?" Jenni asked.

"No," I said. "Why are you asking me that?"

"Your sisters look like Indians or something. Not like you." Jenni was not the first person to ask me that question. There were many before her and would be many after. Instead of explaining that I was half Mexican and there are Mexican's that do have blonde hair and blue eyes, I liked to be a little more creative whenever I answered the question.

"I was born an albino but I started growing out of it," I said

"What is an albino?"

"It is a person with really white skin and pink eyes, like a rabbit, except no fur. Most albinos are blind. I was just lucky."

"I don't believe you," she said. No one really believed the albino story but it was fun to say. I met an albino lady once. Our parents had left us with her family. She taught us how to catch fire flies in jars.

"I was swapped at birth." This was by far my favorite story. "The day I was born, there was a bad storm and it took out all the lights at the hospital. The nurses had to use flashlights to get the babies into their little cribs. By time the lights came back on it was shift change." I could tell Jenni might be buying it. "Two girls born at the exact same time were brought to their mothers who were pretty out of it from the medications and took the babies without question. I was bald so you couldn't tell I had blonde hair. I was sent home with the wrong parents."

"But what about the other kid?"

"I don't know. They probably figured it out by now and are looking for me but we have moved too many times. They will probably never find me."

Jenni studied my face. "Liar," she laughed. Jenni had become my best friend that summer. She lived at the opposite end of our street. She had moved in with her father and stepmother that summer. She had three younger stepsisters and was the youngest of her father's children. Her parents were divorced and she moved in with her dad and stepmom.

Jenni seemed so much older. She had long dark hair with perfectly feathered bangs which she kept in place with a generous application of Aqua Net. Her full lips were perfectly glossed with bubble gum flavored lip balm. She had plucked her eyebrows into thin arches far above her huge brown eyes. I often watched my mother plucking and trimming her own eyebrows into those same thin lines and then coloring them in with a brown pencil. I tried to pluck my eyebrows but it was just too painful and I didn't see the benefit.

"You need to stop wearing those pants," Jenni told me in that superior, I know better than you voice. Her own pants were snug along her hips and down her legs until they spread out at the bottom. They were the same type of bell-bottom pants the hippies across the street wore.

I looked down at my own pants, they were my favorite red corduroys that actually fit me without using a safety pin to hold them up. "What's wrong with them?"

"They are for little kids. Don't wear them anymore." I looked down at the little miniature bunny rabbits printed up and down on both legs. It was in that moment I realized I was no longer a little kid.

I learned how to shave my legs by trial and error. I had watched my mother shave her legs, but really didn't pay attention. My mother never took showers and didn't like to be alone in the bath, so we would sit in the bathroom while she bathed and told us stories of her childhood. She would have us lather up a washcloth and wash her back. Since I got older, now the little kids sit with her.

I borrowed my mom's two-piece bathing suit, which was a little bit big but fit well enough. Jenni and I would take the city bus and go to Point Defiance Park where the older kids would cruise around the five-mile drive showing off cars. Groups gathered and sunbathed by the water, drinking beer hidden in McDonalds cups.

There were a lot of older boys throwing Frisbees to each other across the large grass area on top of the hill right as you entered the park. Jenni had a swish to her walk and I tried to imitate her confidence but she had the right body. I still looked like a kid. We would wave and flirt with the older boys and sometimes they would let us ride around in their cars for the afternoon. We would help them get beer by standing outside the 7-11 and asking a kind looking stranger to buy us beer. Most people said yes, but there was the occasional guy that would get all pissed off and say he was going to tell on us, or "if we were his kids. I look back feeling lucky nothing happened to us.

We spent most of the summer hanging out with each other. I even spent the night with her when it was her mom's weekend. Jenni's mom lived alone in a small house close to the mall, so we'd walk there and hang out.

The mall was where most of the kids our age hung out. We usually didn't have any money, so we just walked around. Occasionally we saw a good-looking set of boys we would follow around until they noticed.

Jenni's mom gave us money to go to the movies. I think she wanted us out of the house. The mall had twin theaters, so we usually had a choice of what movie we wanted to watch. This particular weekend, however, we only had one choice. We were not old enough to get into "Saturday Night Fever", with John Travolta, so we bought tickets to whatever the other movie was and, when nobody was looking, we snuck into "Saturday Night Fever."

At the end of the movie, we walked out not caring who saw us. Instead of going straight home, we found a phone booth and called one of our friends to find out if there were any parties. Soon, we were picked up by two boys Jenni knew from her older brothers. They took us all the way to Puyallup to a high school party. We drank beer and someone gave us a small piece of paper with a purple dot and told us to put it on our tongue. I remember being very paranoid and people moving in slow motion. I don't remember too much more of the rest of the night until the boys were driving us home. I remember I was holding a cup of beer in the backseat with Jenni and one other girl I didn't know. The boys in the front were loudly hippin and hollering with their windows rolled down, harassing other kids in hot rod cars, revving their engines at each other. We were at a red light when I decided to take a drink of my beer and the boys took off and the entire beer was now on my face and all over my front.

When we got back to Jenni's I borrowed a shirt so the next day when my dad came to pick me up he wouldn't smell the beer. I'm not sure how long the acid stays in your system, but the whole ride home, I couldn't concentrate on anything my dad said. His voice was the same voice as the teacher in the Charlie Brown cartoons.

We didn't go to my house too often because my mom was always home. "Your mom doesn't like me," Jenni said.

"She likes you," I said. "She just doesn't smile."

"She looks pissed off."

"I know."

"Plus, your house is always too clean," she said. "I feel like I might mess something up and your mom will get mad." Jenni was right, my mom was constantly cleaning and arranging and rearranging things in the house.

"Mom," I called out, "I'm spending the night at Jenni's."

"Okay," she said from somewhere down the hall. I grabbed a sleeping bag and my small note pad and we left.

It was a clear summer night and we laid our sleeping bags out next to each other. We listened to the top hits on KTAC. In my notebook, I kept track of all the songs that came on the radio so I could figure out the top ten Casey Cason would announce Sunday morning. We took turns running in the house and calling the station, requesting our favorite songs.

I was in love with Andy Gibbs, Jenni loved Sean Cassidy and Teresa loved Leif Garrett. Two people could not have the same one. We wrote and mailed love letters to our famous boy-friends and collected their pictures out of the teen magazines. We had big plans for the future with these teen idols, including marriage and children.

Chapter 14

It was a great summer until tragedy hit Jenni's family. In a terrible accident, Jenni's 21-year-old brother was buried alive while working on a construction site. She was so sad she didn't want anyone around. The loudest, biggest house on the street was now quiet. Jenni just sat in her front yard in a lawn chair and stared into space for days. It was hard to know what to do or say. I never knew anyone who had died. I was sad for Jenni, so I sat on the ground next to her chair, quiet, until she had to go in.

I slowly walked down the sidewalk towards my house, thinking about how horrible it would be if one of my sisters died. As I got closer to the house, I noticed a strange car parked in front next to the neighbor's jeep. It was a brand new white convertible with the top down, exposing the blood red interior.

The strong sent of perfume was the first thing that hit me as I walked through the front door. I followed its trail into the kitchen where I found my mother and Bonnie sitting across from each other at the table, both with coffee cups in their hands.

"There she is," Bonnie said. I was a little shocked, I hadn't seen her in years. She was all grown up.

"Is that your car?" I said shyly. She had basically disappeared when her mother died, and her father sold the house across from Grandma's. There had been rumors about where she had gone, but no one knew for sure. Her hair was curled and a lighter shade of brown than I remembered.

When she stood to give me a hug, I noticed that, even though she was older, she hadn't grown in height. I stood at least six inches above her, but her boobs were way bigger and the shirt she was wearing was cut so she showed a generous amount of cleavage. She had a small cross hanging around her neck on a thin, dainty chain. Her huge brown eyes were a lot like Grandma Nelda's, except Bonnie's were lined with thick black liner and long fake eyelashes, thick with mascara.

Every time she blinked, it seemed like she had to work to reopen them. She also had bright blue eyeshadow all the way up to her thinly lined eyebrows. I had to look carefully but wasn't sure if she even had eyebrows or they were just drawn on. She had pinkish-red blush on both cheeks and bright pink lipstick covered by shiny lip gloss.

Whenever I even put a little bit of eyeshadow on, my dad freaked out and called me a street walker or told me to join the circus. I could imagine what he'd say when he saw Bonnie.

"Bonnie is going to stay with us a while," my mom said and then took a sip of her coffee.

"I am going to share your room, if you don't mind," she said, clapping her hands like a little kid.

"Of course," I said.

"We can hang out just like we used to," she said like a teenager, but she was more like an adult.

My room became Bonnie's personal confessional. I tried not to show shock on my face as she described detailed sexual encounters that she had or when she told me how she had several abortions. She told me she had been sexually abused and she said she had just broken up with a boyfriend who didn't treat her right. I told her about my own adventures, but they paled in comparison. She told me how French kissing and blow jobs were the key to getting and keeping a boyfriend. I had no idea what a blow job was.

"Have you ever French kissed a guy?" she asked.

"Of course. I'm not a child," I said.

"What about a blow job?" she asked.

"Uh, No!" I said, disgusted.

She showed me how to give the best blow job by licking, flicking and moving her tongue around her thumb. I sat watching, trying to be disinterested in what she was saying. I couldn't understand why someone would want to lick a guy's penis. It is where their pee comes out. I felt like I was going to throw up. All Bonnie ever wanted to do was talk about sex—I really didn't. She flirted with every guy we came in contact with, even Uncle Hector.

One night Bonnie put on red lipstick, tight jeans and a short fur coat. She had a date with one of my dad's friends from work. He was way older than her. When she got home the next day she told me they did "it" on the golf course.

The best part of hanging out with Bonnie was that she had her own car and liked to go cruising at the park and had a fake ID so she could buy beer. One afternoon, I came out of the house and she was sitting in the passenger's seat. As soon as I got close enough, she said," You drive."

"I don't know how to drive. I'm not even old enough to get a driver's permit."

"I'll teach you." She opened the passenger's side door and slid in.

"I really don't think this is a good idea." I felt the panic rise in my chest.

"My God! Quit being such a child. Get in. It's about time someone taught you." Like everything else she told me to do, I did it. Against my better judgment, I got in the car. "Move the seat back." She reached under my seat and pulled a lever. "Push." My seat moved back.

"Which foot pedal do I push?"

She rolled her eyes at me. "You are lucky this is an automatic. The right one is gas, the left is brake."

"Gas right, brake left," I repeated several times. I slowly turned the key but held it too long and it made a wicked sound before I let go. The engine was running, and I was now in control.

"Ugg!" She frowned. "Use your mirrors and pull out."

I looked in the rear-view mirror and side mirror and didn't see any other cars. What I did see through the front windshield was cars parked in front of their houses on both sides of the street. It didn't seem like enough room, but people did it every day.

Bonnie grabbed the wheel and turned it slightly. "Put on the gas but pay attention." I did and the car moved. "A little more," she said. I did. She straightened it out and let go. "Now just head straight."

We moved slowly down the street as I over steered a few times and she grabbed the wheel to straighten me out. "Focus ahead more," she said, so I looked ahead to the end of the street. "You are going to make a right turn here," she said as she pointed to the end. I looked at her finger and automatically followed it, turning the wheel as I did. "Brake!" she yelled. I panicked and hit the gas. Before I knew what was happening, the car moved forward, slamming right into a parked Volkswagen.

"Oh shit." I took my foot off the gas and let go of the wheel. Bonnie was out of the car before I could even register what had just happened. She pulled the driver's side door open and pulled me out so hard I almost lost my balance and fell to the ground. I stood back, still in shock, as she got in the car, backed up and took off. From the middle of the road, I watched her go around the same corner we were headed for.

No one came out of their house. No one saw what happened. "I didn't even want to drive," I said out loud to no one.

One thing I knew for sure—I was in a lot of trouble. I walked and then ran the half block to my house and went directly to my bedroom. I laid on my bed waiting for the trouble to start, but it didn't. Bonnie didn't come home that night or the next few nights. I didn't say anything, and nobody seemed to notice she didn't come home.

Bonnie finally showed up wearing cut off shorts and a short crop top with no bra. She was driving a brown and tan station wagon. She had on all her makeup, the bright blue eyeshadow and bright pink lipstick.

"Where is your car?" I wasn't sure if I should ask or not.

"Getting fixed," she said. "Did you say anything?"

"No." I shook my head to make sure she knew I hadn't said anything.

"Let's go for a ride," she said.

"I can't," I told her. "My mom said I need to keep an eye on the girls. They're upstairs playing."

"Teresa can watch them. Let's go to Jubilee." She moved towards me like a cat with her prey. Again, I couldn't stand up to her, and Teresa was probably better at watching the other girls anyway.

She walked out the door and I followed, not bothering to tell anyone where I was going or when I would be home.

"I really am sorry," I said. She glared at me and smiled.

"It was just a stupid accident," she said. I couldn't believe that I got away with it. I wasn't going to get on restriction. Every time either of my parents spoke to me or called my name, I was sure the owner of the Volkswagen had found out it was me who put a huge dent in the front panel of her car.

Jubilee was a popular local hangout with the best messy hamburgers dripping the secret sauce they were famous for. There were a few adults sitting in the booths, but most of the faces were those familiar neighborhood kids we saw at school or riding their bikes down these streets.

We both ordered half chocolate and half vanilla ice cream cones and took a seat across from each other in one of the bright orange plastic booths. I watched the cars pass by on 38th street, trying to avoid eye contact with Bonnie. I licked around the cone, blending the chocolate with the vanilla and stopping any drips. I could feel Bonnie's eyes staring through me as she also licked her cone. I could feel her eyes burning into my head, so I finally turned my attention to her since it was now obvious she had something to say.

"You knew that Jose isn't your real father, didn't you?" I watched her fake eyelashes move up and down like butterfly wings, slow and deliberate as I tried to register what she just said. Her big brown eyes watched me carefully, looking for a crack. The wry smile and bent head reminded me of a snake moving back and forth.

Did she just say Jose was not my real father? Yes. That is exactly what she said. There was no way I would give this bitch the satisfaction of an emotional breakdown. With the words still echoing in my brain, "…not your real father…," I matched her tight smile and blinked my lashes in time with hers. She was Muhamad Ali and I was Joe Frazer. Her first strike had landed as a direct hit straight to the gut because I wasn't paying attention. But I didn't go down. I was as weak as she thought, but I was strategic and took my time.

I started to laugh but it quickly turned into more of a hysterical cackle that I couldn't control. I choked down the tears, but not before a few had found their way down my hot cheeks. I quickly wiped away the evidence, but she saw it. She saw it all. The exact response she wanted. I was in shock.

A few of the people turned to look at me when I laughed but lost interest as their own conversations were more interesting than whatever was going on in our booth.

"Of course, I knew. I'm not stupid." The words came out fractured and too loud. Her smile said she didn't believe me. All the years, all the questions, all the denials. It was true... I knew it in my gut. Everyone in my life was a liar. Immediately all I could think about was escape. I needed away from this person. I walked away from her, dropped the rest of the cone in the garbage and walked home.

My mom was just hanging up the phone when I walked in. "Guess who that was?" I didn't care. "Bonnie." She must have used the corner phone booth and called my house after I left.

"I don't care." I was still numb, and I was now face to face with the biggest liar of all. This was the person who would pull out the birth certificate and show me who my father was.

"She said you wrecked her car?"

"Yeah, I did, like a week ago. It was her fault, she made me drive and I didn't want to."

"Funny, that's what I told her. She shouldn't have let you drive."

"You know what she told me?" I stood face to face with my mother, staring straight into her blue eyes. I watched the half smile slowly change as her panic grew.

"What?" Her voice was weak and low.

"Who is my father?" I started to cry. She just stood there.

"Where is he? Do you even know who he is?" I was becoming loud and anxious.

"I...I...I'm so sorry." Now she was crying and about to go into one of her breakdowns. I wasn't going to let her put a guilt trip on me today.

I was confused. My teenage brain was having a hard time processing the information Bonnie had just told me, which was more than likely a confirmation of suspicions that lived in the deepest part of my brain most of my life. I replayed so many conversations with people who commented on how different I looked from all my sisters. Had I just refused to hear the truth?

I've witnessed my mother having breakdowns many times over things I didn't always understand. My mother was fragile like an antique china tea cup—if you handled it a little rough, it might crack. When she cracked, she disappeared into her bedroom and slept for days.

But today, I didn't care. I didn't consider the consequences, the rage that welled up in my soul was just too great to hold back. If I was going to deal with this it would be this moment.

"You're a fucking liar," I screamed. Her shock was instant and froze her where she stood. Her blue eyes wide with shock turned quickly to fire as her lip curled, and her free hand flew to the side of my face where the slap was so loud it froze time. She dropped the cup of coffee, which must not have been too hot since she didn't move as it spilled all the way down her pants. The next few minutes happened in slow motion. Her mouth was open in a wide "o" and, before she could say a thing, I turned and ran to my room, slamming the door.

I looked in the mirror and stared. I touched my hair. My eyes were so blue, my nose was so straight. My lips were thin like my mother's, but I didn't look like my mother. Who do I look like? But more importantly, who am I? Does my brain look different than the other people in my family? I have always felt like I belonged somewhere else. I was an outsider, and I missed my real family.

Chapter 15

My room was at the back of the house and the window faced the back yard. My sisters were playing outside, and I could see they had mixed water and dirt and were making mud pies. They already had several pie-sized lumps formed on the cement. Their world was still innocent, while my world had been rocked—my life exposed as a complete lie. How was I going to face my dad, not my dad, but the man who has been pretending to be my dad?

I couldn't stay there, but I didn't know where to go. I put a few things into a pillow case and walked out the back door. My mom was in her room, probably crying, but I didn't care. I hated her guts and I would never forgive her. I walked past the girls and they barely noticed me go by. I ran and ran until I was finally out of breath and my legs failed. I sat down on the sidewalk with my head between my knees. Finally, I cried. I cried tears of betrayal. I cried because I hurt my mother and she had slapped me. The self-pity overwhelmed me. Why did everything have to happen to me? Why couldn't I have a normal life with normal parents?

I couldn't go home, so I found a bus stop and waited for whatever bus showed up. My city bus pass could take me anywhere, even if I just wanted to ride around a while. I only waited a few minutes to board the bus that was going to the mall, but I wasn't in the mall mood so I got off at the transfer station downtown. It was summer and unusually hot for the Pacific Northwest, so the breeze was not refreshing but rather suffocating as I walked down Broadway for a while.

Maybe my real father had a new wife and kids and had been looking for me all these years. If I could get more information, I could find him. I sat at the transfer station and watched buses come and go. One of the bus placards said "North End". Uncle Hector lived in the North End, so I boarded the bus, carrying my pillowcase. I sat in the very back, watching out the window for anything that looked familiar. As soon as I saw the big high school we always drove by when my dad drove us, I got off the bus. It turned out to be a little farther than I thought but, somehow, I found the house.

Homes in the North End were bigger and farther apart than in the neighborhoods on the Southside, where we lived. Most of the houses there had trimmed green grass and baskets of flowers hanging on large front porches. The front doors welcomed you with fancy door knockers and leaded windows. Uncle Hector's front door was thick, dark oak with a stained-glass window at the very top as decoration. As I knocked, I wasn't even a hundred percent sure I was at the right house or that anyone would be home. Just as the fear almost shook my confidence, Aunt Kathy opened the door, obviously surprised to see me. She smiled and looked beyond me, searching the street, probably looking for whoever had brought me to her doorstep.

"What are you doing here?" she asked, a little confused but not hostile. Aunt Kathy was quite a bit shorter than me with short grey hair and big round glasses. She wore a bit of pink lipstick but no other makeup. Their two Doberman Pinschers stood behind her but didn't react.

"I ran away." I just said it when I realized that is exactly what I did. I ran away from home. No one knew where I went, but they probably didn't care.

"Oh," she said and stood aside. "Well you better come in then." I hadn't realized it, but I was holding my breath. I could finally breathe, suddenly exhausted. The adrenalin from the day was starting to dissipate. I took another deep breath—the house smelled like brownies.

There was something so comforting about my aunt's and uncle's house. The brown overstuffed couch and two well used blue easy chairs took up the space in front of a dusty television set. Family pictures took up all the wall space in the hallway. The stairs that led up to three bedrooms and a bathroom had a large landing with a giant picture of a Mexican bullfighter on one wall and some type of metal family crest hanging on another. An armor-clad figure half as tall as I was stood guard in the corner.

A large oak table and matching cupboard took up most of the space in the dining room. Decorative plates were hung across the tops of the walls. On one wall hung a giant wooden fork and spoon.

Every window had heavy burgundy curtains with gold fringe. They were tied back with thick golden ropes like what you might see at the theater.

All the windows were open, creating a slight breeze through the house, causing what I called invisible snow—those tiny dust particles that could only be seen in the right sunlight. Aunt Kathy sat in her chair and picked up the crochet she must have been working on when I arrived. I sunk into the side of the couch closest to her.

Aunt Kathy was not like most adults. She really listened and gave you her honest opinion. She wasn't afraid to say anything.

It was quite a surprise when we met Aunt Kathy and she was not the Chinese woman Uncle Hector had described. She was an older white lady with short brown-greyish hair in no particular style. She was much different than Uncle Hector's first wife, Aunt Rena. Aunt Kathy was 16 years older than uncle Hector and had four children. Two boys were still at home but were almost finished with high school. I instantly loved Aunt Kathy. She was so easy to talk to. She liked to read and sew like I did. We had a lot in common. Sometimes I wished she could be my mother.

"So, what's going on?" She was looking at me, but her fingers were busy with the double crochet in her lap. I wished I had some yarn and a hook in my own hands. My hands were sweaty and I kept them clasped together on my lap.

"Did you know that my dad wasn't my real dad?" I finally asked.

"Yes." her fingers stopped moving and she looked right at me like she was trying to figure out if she should say more.

"Does everyone know?" I was a little surprised when she said yes. Who told her? Did she ask someone or was it just obvious? I couldn't understand my own feelings at this point was I pissed or embarrassed?

She shook her head. "I don't know. I am so sorry." Her fingers started back to busily wrapping around the yarn and pulling through as the afghan, or whatever the project was, kept growing without her even looking at what she was doing.

"When did you find out?" I asked.

"I have known your dad for many years," she confessed. "Your dad and I worked together even before I met your uncle. We actually were very good friends, and I knew about all you girls, including you and Teresa."

"Teresa?" I said it aloud because Bonnie had told me that too, but I dismissed it because Teresa was brown and looked like the other girls. I was the one who didn't belong to this family.

"Both you and Teresa were already born when your mom and dad met."

"That doesn't make sense," I said, "she is Mexican like my dad." I already knew that Teresa had a different father because Bonnie tried to trick me. The image of the ridiculous smirk on her face was burned into my skull.

"I guess her father must have also been Mexican."

"But not mine." It wasn't a question, just a statement that came out instead of staying in my head.

"Obviously, not yours." She smiled a reassuring smile.

"What's goin' on?" His words came out flat. Normally when Uncle Hector came in the room, he took it over. His "what's going on?" made you smile. He was loud and happy. I don't think I had ever seen him in a serious mood before this minute.

"I ran away," I said confidently. "I am not going back."

"I told Jose and Bernice they should have told you a long time ago." He sat next to me and put his arm around my shoulders. I could feel a hot tear rolling down my cheek. I quickly wiped it away. I was making him sad.

"I'm sorry," I said. "I didn't know where to go. I don't know what to do."

"It's okay," he said. "I already talked to your dad. I guess your mom is pretty upset."

"Did you know my real dad?" I asked him.

"No." He shook his head. "That was way before I knew your mom. Your mom was pregnant with Lisa when I moved to Washington."

"Did you know that I had a different dad than my sisters?"

"Charisse, it was pretty obvious, but no one ever said anything and, if the subject came up, your parents made it very clear that it was not okay to talk about, especially in front of you girls. However, I don't think your father, Jose, has treated you different than any of the other girls."

"They still lied. I flat out asked the question and they said I was Mexican." The fury was building again, but I held on to my emotions.

"I think they are ready to be honest now," he said. "I told your dad I would bring you home. I understand if you are having a hard time, but I think the best thing to do is to go talk to them. It probably won't be easy but it is the right thing to do."

"I really don't think that's a good idea. I think I want to stay here." I had no idea how my mom would be feeling right now. I had never seen my mom so upset before and it was all my fault. My dad was probably furious with me. He didn't like it when my mom was upset.

As we drove to my house on the Southside, we passed the government housing where we used to live. I remembered how happy we were when we moved into that house, to have indoor plumbing and heat you could just turn on. Uncle Hector wasn't around very much in those days. I was glad I had him back in my life. He was stability.

When I turned 13, he and Aunt Kathy took just me to Barb-B-Que Pete's for dinner. It was the fanciest dinner I had ever been to. The waiter stood up on the chair and dropped honey over his back, right into the dish on our table. Another time, he took all us girls to K-Mart and bought us each something. I got a pair of bellbottom jeans. Those were my favorite jeans and I wore them every day. I wanted to be just like Uncle Hector when I was an adult. But that was when it hit me, if my dad wasn't my dad, Uncle Hector wasn't my uncle. Hot tears flooded my eyes. My whole life was ruined.

We walked up to the front door like unwanted strangers. The door and the people behind it were unrecognizable. Uncle Hector knocked on the door, even though I could have just walked in since I actually lived there, but he had the lead on this one. I stood back, not knowing what to expect.

My dad opened the door and his brown face was pale and his dark eyes were tired. Behind him, sitting on the couch, was an unrecognizable woman who resembled my mother. Her Clairol Red #8, normally carefully styled, was like a rat's nest, which was her term when my hair wasn't brushed out. The roots barely showed her natural mousy brown color, very different from my blonde. Her blue-green eyes were red rimmed with dark circles. Her makeup was nonexistent except for the black streaks she hadn't bothered to wipe off, maybe for effect, maybe not. Her thin lips were two tight flat lines intent not to speak. I was thankful she didn't make eye contact with any of us. Uncle Hector and my father both sat on the couch next to my mother. I stood with my back to the door in case I needed to run.

I had never really noticed how cold this room was. This furniture and this house were so different from anywhere we had lived before. It was all a result of my father having a real job where he went to work every day. The white walls were bare except for a metal art piece centered over the modern white couch, which was protected by a clear plastic cover. The glass coffee table sat lonely in the center of the room. This was the first time I even remember anyone sitting on this couch. The two lamps that stood guard on each side of the couch lit up the room like a medical facility. The only thing that was missing was a straitjacket and two white clad guards.

"I think Charisse is just feeling hurt." As soon as Uncle Hector spoke, my mother started to moan like a hurt animal. She had a handful of her thick red hair. My father reached over and peeled her fingers out of the tangled mess as Uncle Hector stood up. It was obvious this was a bad idea.

"You should have told her," he said. My mother looked up at him with hate in her eyes. I had never seen her this discomposed. There was one time when my parents had gone out drinking and my father brought her home and got me out of bed to come take care of her so he could go back out. I sat on her bed with her as she talked like a baby, repeating herself about how sorry she was and how she didn't want me to see her like this. I remember being terrified—a lot like I was in this moment.

Uncle Hector looked over at me, clearly recognizing my uneasiness. No words were necessary. I walked out the door and went directly to his truck, where I stood frozen. I heard some loud sounds and my uncle saying something. He came out and we left.

Neither of us said a word as we drove back to his house. My mind again went over the fact that he wasn't my uncle. If he knew this fact all my life, or rather since I was a toddler, why was he so nice to me? It seemed like he treated me just like my sisters. Why didn't he tell me? He seemed so normal.

When we got to the house, Aunt Kathy had a pot roast along with potatoes and carrots sitting on the table for dinner. How did she know this was my favorite meal?

The next day, I called Grandma Nelda on the phone.

"Bonnie told me. Why didn't you tell me? There were so many times you could have told me."

"I thought, when the time was right, your mom and dad would have told you." I looked at my watch. It was only 10 am, so she wasn't drunk yet. "I did tell you that you weren't like the rest of them."

"Do you know my real dad?"

"His name is Gene or Eugene, I don't really remember. He was in the Army, stationed at Fort Lewis. Did you ask your mom?"

"I can't talk to her. She gets upset. I want to know the truth."

"Bernice has a tender heart. I tell you, I had to run the man off. He came to the house to see you and he tried to kill your mom. He had his hands wrapped around her neck. I poked my shotgun right to his chest. Never seen him again."

"Where did he go?"

"Probably back to his mama somewhere in Wisconsin." I heard her suck in a long breath, obviously lighting another cigarette and then releasing it into the phone. "You need to go home."

"I'm not going home." I was defeated. She wasn't going to tell me anything and, anyway, I wouldn't know if it was the truth or not.

Chapter 16

Jessica Gonzalas was a special education teacher at Mary Lyon Elementary school, who focused on issues unique to the growing Hispanic population in Tacoma public schools. The children spent a few hours in her class learning to assimilate into the main stream.

For some reason, probably their last name or a checkmark on their school registration, Josette and Lisa were identified as part of this disadvantaged group and were brought into this special class. The real disadvantage they now faced was that they were the only kids in the program who didn't know how to speak Spanish.

It was a rare event when one or both of our parents came to 'back to school night,' but this year they did. Each of us led them around our classrooms, showing off our work and listening to each teacher say what wonderful children we were.

Josette's teacher was a large, redheaded woman with bright red lipstick. The kids all called her Gorilla Butt because she had a huge behind.

"Are you sure Josette should be missing class to go to this special program?" my mom asked.

"It's not like she is going to college," Gorilla Butt said. "I actually think it will help with her disadvantages."

"What disadvantages?" my dad spoke up. My mom stood in shock that the teacher could say that about a second grader. How could she even identify potential at this age?

"I think the Focus on Heritage program will make a difference," the teacher said smugly. She obviously thought brown skin was an instant disadvantage. "I believe our program director is here tonight in room 2B if you would like to discuss this." She walked away towards the next set of parents.

Room 2B was on the opposite side of the school in a temporary metal building with the words Annex 2B on it. It was right next to an identical building, Annex 2A, where we went for music class. The classroom had six desks arranged in a half circle instead of in rows. There was one other family on their way out as we filed in behind my parents.

"Welcome. Buenos Notches." Mrs. Gonzalas was a young Latino woman. She had long black hair pulled into a pony tail that was almost down to her waist. She wasn't wearing any makeup, but her smile lit up her face. All of us girls took a seat at one of the desks, leaving only one chair vacant. We watched the three adults like they were performing for us.

That is when the Spanglish started up. That is what we called it when half the sentence was in Spanish and half English. We were used to it because that is how Uncle Hector and our dad spoke. Mom stood silent but paid close attention. She didn't like it when she was left out, but listened like we'd be able to catch the overall conversation.

What we figured out was that, "The girls didn't quite fit the overall goal of the class, but why not let them participate because it was good that they are exposed to others in their nationality. It wasn't hurting them." The real reason was probably that she had a minimum participation requirement to keep the program at the school, which determined whether she had a job or not. Josette and Lisa represented one third of the class. I would find out later that Mrs. Gonzalas's two boys were also in the class.

Sunday was usually filled with football and the newspaper. My dad let me have the funny pages and the editorials as he would read the rest. But this Sunday we all dressed up and went to church. This church was not like any church we had ever attended—it wasn't Easter and it wasn't Catholic.

The church was located not too far from our house on a large corner lot. It looked like it was a converted house. It was blue with a large white wooden cross attached to the front. There was one of those rectangular type plastic signs that said, "Apostolic Assembly" and had a large section underneath where you could move around plastic letters for a different message every week. This week it just said "Acts 2:38".

Mrs. Gonzalas was at the door to greet us. She led us to one of the long pews where our family took up almost the whole row. We watched as the church filled up all around us with other Mexican families. Everyone smiled and greeted us in Spanish. My dad spoke to everyone in their language.

One of the last families to arrive was led by a very tall white man with a tall white wife holding a white baby girl and followed by four white boys. They were Henry and Henrietta Hordike and their "H" named children. They looked out of place, because they were white, but the mother was dressed exactly like the other women in the church. They took the first row, closest to the pulpit and, like us, took up most of the row.

All the women in this church had long hair, and most of them had it wrapped around into giant piles on top of their heads. The younger girls and teens all wore their hair down. Most of them had hair down to their butts. There was a woman standing in the row in front of us with hair that was down to her knees. I couldn't help wondering how she sat on the toilet without the hair falling in. All the women also wore small head coverings they called veils. These veils were not like a veil a bride wore, which covered the face, but were small pieces of cloth or netting pinned in order to cover the top of the head.

All the women in the church, except in our family, were wearing dresses. All of them had sleeves to their wrists and skirts that hung below their knees. Some of them wore tennis shoes with their dresses, which I thought odd. The men all had short hair and were dressed in shirts and ties.

"Welcome Brother and Sister Orona and their beautiful family," the tall white man said from behind the pulpit. He was the assistant pastor. My dad gave a small wave. I slunk down as everyone turned to welcome us in a mix of Spanish and English.

"Let us pray." He led the congregation in a loud prayer that had a lot of audience participation. This definitely wasn't a Catholic Church, where you needed to be quiet. The white man was just the warm up act and turned over the church to the main pastor, who was "Brother" Jon Gonzalas, Mrs. Gonzalas's husband.

Jon Gonzalas was short in stature but a force for God. He didn't need a microphone and came down from behind the pulpit. "Can I get an 'Amen'," he yelled.

"Amen!" came from all around us.

He preached the "Word of God" in both Spanish and English, and I was bored.

"Can I get a Witness?" he yelled. The whole time he moved back and forth across the platform, hands raised, his jet-black hair didn't move. It was so shiny and perfect, it didn't look real. He wore a white-collared shirt but I could see that he wore a short sleeved white T-shirt underneath. Where that t-shirt ended, I could make out that his arms were covered with tattoos, some that peeked out at the wrists.

All of a sudden, the church went silent and a woman somewhere behind me was speaking loudly in a language that I knew was not Spanish and definitely not English. The whole church had one or both of their hands in the air whispering, "yes Lord" or "Amen". For some reason, I was scared. I didn't like the tone of her voice, it sounded like she was possessed.

When she was finished, another woman stood and translated what was apparently a message straight from God. The first woman was speaking in "tongues," God's language. Later it would be explained to me. The only way to get to heaven was to be baptized in Jesus's name, ask forgiveness for all your sins and be able to speak in tongues. The message in the front of the church now made sense—"Acts 2:38: Then Peter said unto them, Repent, and be baptized every one of you in the name of Jesus Christ for the remission of sins, and ye shall receive the gift of the Holy Ghost." The gift of the Holy Ghost was speaking in tongues.

The rest of the three or four hours was more of the same, singing, clapping, crying, amen-ing, witnessing and falling on the ground. I guess this is why people referred to this type of church as "Holy Rollers."

On the ride home, we were silent until my mom said, "That was crazy. I'm not going back." I sat back in relief.

It didn't take long before they were fully immersed in the Church of the Apostolic Assembly and the lifestyle that went with it, including getting rid of our TV, only wearing dresses, not cutting hair, no makeup and no jewelry. The one thing my mom refused to comply with was taking off her wedding ring. It was just a simple gold band, but she said it represented something important to her.

It seemed like the major debate among the churches was whether Jesus was God. Is Jesus God or God's son? I pointed out that most Christian's plastered John 3:16 on their bumpers. "For God so loved the world that he gave his only begotten Son, that whosoever believeth in him should not perish, but have everlasting life."

My point was that it didn't make sense to take one verse of the bible over another as the "rule". Jon says all I have to do is believe in God and I can live forever. I was constantly trying to pick apart the reasoning they were using to convince me to go along with the program. I refused. I would not stop wearing pants, I would cut my bangs and continue to wear make-up.

"How about the tribes in Africa who have never even seen a white person or heard of Jesus Christ?" My mom explained that because they didn't know the truth, they would still go to heaven, but that is why the Church sends missionaries around the world to educate and save the people through the "Truth". It seemed to me that more people would get into heaven if everybody would just leave them alone.

The new church took over our lives. We not only had church for four hours every Sunday but there were full services on Wednesday night and bible studies every Tuesday and Friday.

After Sunday service, outside the small blue church with a large white cross nailed to the front, small groups of parishioners gathered in fellowship on the dried grass lawn instead of rushing home. Younger children, dressed in their Sunday best, chased each other around the church and weaved in and out of the adults. Several young mothers, who didn't look even close to 18 and spoke only Spanish, gathered together, holding babies in their arms, bouncing and rocking to keep them busy. The kids my age were all part of the youth group that stayed in the church, planning a day trip to Mt. Rainer the following weekend. "Veils are stupid." I said to my mother.

"In order to honor God, you must cover your head," my mother said. She was wearing a veil that Sister Hordike had given her.

It looked like a fancy handkerchief cut into a circle and was pinned to my mom's head with big black bobby pins. My mother had already stopped wearing make-up and cutting her hair, so she looked pale and plain like the other women, except her skin was whiter than the rest.

Sister Gonzalas was standing close enough to hear our conversation. "I Corinthians 11: Verses 5 and 6 says 'But every woman who prays or prophesies with her head uncovered dishonors her head—it is the same as having her head shaved." "For if a woman does not cover her head, she might as well have her hair cut off; but if it is a disgrace for a woman to have her hair cut off or her head shaved, then she should cover her head." Sister Gonzalas knew the verses by heart. She was a short, pretty woman with a pile of black hair wrapped in a giant bun on her head, like most of the women in the group. I wondered how long her hair was if she let it down. If these women never cut their hair, did it touch the floor?

Later, when I looked up the passage for myself, I was interested to find that men were not to cover their heads, and Verse 14 says, "Doth not even nature itself teach you, that, if a man have long hair, it is a shame unto him?" All the pictures of Jesus and his disciples showed them with long hair. I was definitely going to bring up this fact. It was obvious that I was going to have to read the whole bible in order to stand up for myself.

I would look up every rule and make my pitch about how none of it made any sense. Finally, my parents gave up and the only thing I really had to do was to go to church on Sunday with the family. Every Sunday, it was a huge fight between my father and me, and on one occasion he had physically dragged me to the car.

I did decide to wear a veil to church. If it would save my eternal soul, it was a good thing, but more importantly I saw a great money-making opportunity.

I went to the fabric store and bought some tulle, which was just simple netting that I could cut into various-sized circles and embroider flowers or other designs on them and sell them to the sisters. I charged $5 apiece. The Sisters loved them, and I sold as many as I could make. I even made little girl and baby sizes.

Even though I was only required to go to church on Sundays, my parents, pastor and members of the youth group constantly put pressure on me to go to youth group on Friday night.

I made a deal with my dad that I would go to youth group if he bought me a pair of jeans from the mall. Somehow my father decided that my soul would be better off at church, so as an enticement, he decided to relax the "no pants" rule. A miracle happened—he took me to the mall, we found a store that specialized in cool jeans, and he bought me a pair of "San Francisco Riding Gear-Double Belts" and a pair of "Star Jeans". I was finally going to be a normal teenager.

I held up my part of the bargain and went to youth group. It was totally boring and stupid. Sometimes I could get one of my friends to go with me. Brother Jon and his wife were pretty involved with the youth, so they were around a lot. For some reason, they both took a liking to me and went out of their way to chat with me whenever possible.

"Got anything for me today?" Brother Jon would ask me. I think he thought the more I questioned, sooner or later he would be able to convince me of "the Truth." The truth was, I saw way too many holes in their whole belief system and whenever I did ask a question, the answer was not a real answer, and most of the time included the phrase, "you've got to have faith."

Often people would Testify in front of the church, which was sort of a confession of where you were and how you came to the lord. His testimony was my favorite. He had been a drug dealer in a gang in Los Angeles and he had spent some time in jail. The devil was dragging him down until one night an angel came to him with a message. "It is not your destiny to take life but to save eternal lives through your words and leadership. You are responsible for those souls." Now I was one of those souls.

At the end of the service, anyone who needed prayer would come to the front of the church to have hands laid upon then. The more experienced would lay their hands on the person's shoulders or on their back.

The pastor or assistant pastor would shout "In Jesus Name!" and forcefully grab their head with both hands. "Heal my sister!" or brother, but mostly sisters participated. The person faints and falls to the floor. Women on standby rush over to the woman lying on the floor and cover her legs with a baby blanket as the pastor moves to the next person. The process continues until all the sufferers are on the floor.

Since I didn't go to church on Wednesday nights, I missed the time the pastor cast the devil out of a possessed man who had once been a good Christian. He had lost his job and marriage because he could not stop doing drugs and sleeping with women. The brothers gathered around him and laid hands on him until the demon came out through the man's mouth. He described the demon as a long green fire that fell to the floor before it rolled down the center of the church and out the door, into the world to find a new victim. Backsliders were the most vulnerable of all people for being taken over by a bad spirit because they knew Jesus and turned away.

Chapter 17

The signs of the times were telling us that the end of the world was close, and I began to believe some of the teachings. I figured it wouldn't hurt to get baptized, so one Sunday, wearing a white dress bought for the occasion, I lined up with a few other kids my age.

We took turns walking down three steps into a large tub that was usually covered during normal services but today was filled with about three feet of lukewarm water. The pastor stood in the water in loose, white pants and a white dress shirt, the sleeves rolled up to his elbows. "Do you confess your sins and turn your life over to Jesus Christ?" the Pastor said.

I stood in front of him. "Yes," I said and moved beside him where he grabbed my head and shouted, "In Jesus Name!" as he dunked me back into the water. The shock of the water and the praise of the church got ahold of me. I raised my hands and tears flowed from my eyes. I was given a towel as I came out the other side of the large baptism tub. I was saved. I could now go to heaven if I died.

My salvation didn't last very long, and I was never able to "speak in tongues", which is one of the requirements to go to Heaven. I wasn't going to give up wearing pants or earrings. I just didn't fit into my family no matter how much I tried. I would always be the outsider. I had to figure out a way to make some money so I could hire a private investigator to find my real father.

All of us girls liked to work and make money. Even as young as 6 and 7 years old, Teresa and I helped my dad bundle wood kindling so he could sell to the local 7-11 stores. We would cut tire inner tubes into half inch circles, like giant rubber bands, and take a piece of seasoned wood and, using a small ax, split the smaller pieces. Once we had ten or twelve small pieces, we would wrap the inner tube band around them to hold them secure. My dad would pay us 10 cents for each bundle. At that point, we didn't have much of a concept of money, but I remember being able to save up enough dimes that I could buy a set of jacks.

When I was old enough, I had a paper route. I had to get up early in the morning while it was still dark out, rain or shine, and pick up my pile of papers from the distribution point, fold them just right, and if it was raining, stuff them into clear plastic bags. I walked the blocks wearing my special newspaper vest that got lighter with every paper I threw onto someone's porch. I only lasted a few months because of collections. I didn't mind the delivery, but when I had to go door to door collecting money for that month, some people just refused to pay. I wasn't tough enough to make them pay, so it came out of the money I should have made. It wasn't worth it.

In another endeavor, I printed my name and phone number on three-by-five cards and distributed these through the neighborhood, advertising myself available for babysitting at $1 an hour. I had a few weekend gigs, but for an entire summer, I babysat for Shawn and Rachel while their mother worked.

When I wasn't babysitting, I would also go door to door in our neighborhood collecting aluminum cans and old newspapers to recycle. When I had a large garbage bag or two full of aluminum, I would borrow my sisters' little red wagon and transport the bags to the Reynolds Recycling Center.

After all that effort, I finally had enough money to hire a detective. I met with Jill Smith, a private investigator specializing in finding parents and children of adoption. I didn't think it was necessary to tell anyone how old I was when I made the appointment. She explained the process that she would go through and was fairly confident that she could locate my father.

"Sometimes the parent doesn't want to be found," she said. "I will call first and then find out if he would be willing to speak with you. I'm telling you this because you need to be prepared for the worst." I heard her words, but I knew that he would want to see me. As soon as my father knew where I was, he would come and visit. I had always wanted a brother, maybe I had more sisters. "If he is married and has another family, he may not want to connect."

"I understand," I told her and handed her $300 dollars that I had saved for this.

"It could take up to six months," she said.

I told her, "His name was Gene McFarlin and he was from Wisconsin and he was in the Army stationed at Fort Lewis in 1963 where I was born at Madigan Army Hospital. I really don't know more and can't really ask my mother."

"That should be enough," she assured me.

Instead of catching the bus, I decided to walk home. I was too excited to sit still. I would finally see where I got my thin nose, blonde hair and blue eyes. I might finally feel a connection I so longed for. I would finally find the family I was supposed to be born into.

Several weeks went by when Jill called me. "I need another $200," she said. "Because you are not 18, I have to go about this another way." I took her word for it and took her $180, which was all I had, promising to get her the last $20 when I could.

Every few weeks, I called her and she gave me some excuse and I started getting frustrated. "I told you it would take up to six months," she said. She assured me she had filed the papers she needed, requesting documents like my original birth certificate be released.

The next time I talked to Jill, she had bad news. "The state won't release your records because of your age. We are going to have to wait until you are 18."

"But what about the extra $200?" I asked.

"It was worth a try," she said. "It just didn't work out… These things happen…," I felt hot tears running down my face. This was my only hope. I would never find my father. I would feel this lost for the rest of my life.

I was so depressed and lost—I would never find my real family. I went home and slammed the door to my bedroom. I took out a joint I had stashed in my bottom dresser drawer under my pants and checked the door to make sure it was locked. I lit the joint and blew the smoke out the window I had opened. I just wanted to stay high all the time.

IX

1978: Charisse (Age 15)

Chapter 18

Chong's was a small convenience store on 56th where we could buy beer without showing ID or begging a stranger to buy it for us, risking that they would just keep the money. One Friday night Lulu, Dawn and I went into Chong's, paid for a case of beer, and drove around the back to pick it up. When it was dark, we drove to Wapato Park where we met up with a group of boys from our school.

I sat against a large fir tree drinking my beer when the tall figure of Richard Thayer, my sixth-grade crush, was standing right in front of me.

"What are you doing here, blondie?" He was even more handsome than I remembered, with his unruly blond hair and sexy smile. He sat next to me and my heart almost jumped out of my chest, but the beer had given me some courage.

"You know I have had a crush on you since sixth grade."

"Really." He smiled. "Why didn't you ever say anything?" he said, leaning in close.

"I'm shy," I said, tilting my head close to his. I could smell the beer on his breath. He took the hint and kissed me. It was everything I had imagined it would be, his tongue was smooth and slow, but not too slow, as it explored my entire mouth. He sent chills up my spine when he kissed my neck at the same time he reached under my shirt and found my bra and expertly snapped it undone, giving him full access to my breasts. His soft fingers made my stomach fill with butterflies. It was when he reached down to the top button of my jeans that I stopped him by whispering, "I'm on my period."

He pulled back and smiled. "I don't care. I've earned my wings." I didn't know what the hell he was talking about, but I started to panic.

"I care," I said and took a drink of my beer. I guess the fun was over since he went to get another beer and disappeared.

When I got home, I noticed three hickeys on my neck. There was no way I was going to hide them. I put mint toothpaste on the marks hoping by the morning they would be gone. Morning came and the hickeys looked worse than the night before. I was tempted to use my curling iron and burn myself and say it was burn marks but they were on both sides of my neck. Instead I wore a turtleneck and got away with it until Sunday when my dad spotted them.

"What is on your neck?" my father said.

"Curling iron burns," I said.

"I'm not stupid—those are hickeys. Who gave you hickeys?" he said.

"Actually, my friends thought they were funny Friday night when I spent the night at Lulu's. They held me down and used the vacuum. I told them I was going to get in trouble but they didn't care."

"You are on restriction until those hickeys are gone," he said. "Do you want people to think you are a slut? Because sluts are the only ones that walk around like that."

I was on restriction a lot, but I didn't really mind because I liked hanging out in my room reading a book. I hated my family, so I avoided them as much as possible.

At school, I saw Richard making out with Kim, his old girlfriend. I guess they got back together. It seemed like no boys were ever going to like me. The last day of the school year, I got back at him by letting all the air out of his tires when it was parked in the student parking lot.

I stopped going to church and my father finally gave up making me. It wasn't as simple as that, since the last time he tried to get me to go to church, he had to physically drag me into the car where I struggled, and as soon as he got in the front seat, I got out.

He got out again and chased me to the front porch. "You hate me, don't you?" I yelled at him. For some reason that stopped him in his tracks.

He looked me straight in the eye and said," I hate what you do…" He said some other stuff but I didn't hear any of it. All I wanted to hear is that he hated me. My ears burned and I now had a reason to hate him back.

My sisters and mom were all in shock and didn't move from the car, where they all sat quiet. I saw their faces and I felt sad for making them sad, but I was done with this family. I walked down the block, since the house was locked and I didn't have a key, leaving my dad standing there. When I finally turned around, the car was gone.

Because I was so withdrawn and acting out, my mother took me to a psychologist. What she didn't know was that I was actually planning my death. I was so depressed and sad, I felt lost and defeated. I wanted to commit suicide but I was too afraid to slit my wrists even though I knew that you have to cut them vertically. —the people who cut horizontally just want attention. I couldn't hang myself, I would never be brave enough. I had no gun available, but again, I don't think I would have been brave enough to pull the trigger. I tried to drown myself in the bathtub but I couldn't keep my head under long enough. I would probably just take pills and just go to sleep—if I knew where to get enough of that kind of pills. I had tried to take a bunch of aspirin but it just made me have a stomach ache and throw up.

When we got to the psychiatrist's office, I sat on the opposite side of the room from my parents. My mom sat in the chair next to my dad with her head down like a wounded animal. My dad picked up whatever magazine sat on top of a fanned-out pile and was flipping through the pages looking for something interesting to read.

A bald man opened his office door to greet us. He had sideburns and a thick mustache but no beard, so he looked like a walrus. He wore wire rimmed glasses he probably didn't even need, but wore just to look smart. Psychiatrists were not real doctors, and I would prove it.

His office was smaller than I imagined. Three of the walls were bookshelves, full of books, all the way up to the ceiling. He had a small desk stacked with papers and file folders, probably with all his poor desperate clients' life stories. He had me pick where to sit. I had a choice of a small two-person couch or an oversized leather chair. Of course, I chose the chair. I was not going to get too comfortable.

I matched his fake smile with my own.

"Blah, blah, blah," he said.

I shook my head no, then nodded yes. He looked at me completely confused.

"How about we try a relaxation technique?" he suggested.

"Sure." I didn't roll my eyes but thought, "Oh brother!"

"Are you comfortable?" he asked.

"Yes." I said flatly. My brain said, "NO!"

"What I want you to do is sit back against the back of the chair, close your eyes and breath normally." He waited a few minutes as I fought to keep my eyes closed. "Now I want you to take a deep breath and think about your feet and relax your toes. Now concentrate on your ankles, relax your ankles. Take a deep breath and feel your knees, blah, blah, blah. Now concentrate on the top of your head and let all the tension run out of your body. Take a deep breath."

I took a deep breath and let it out loudly.

"Now I don't want you to talk but I want you to respond to me using your index finger on your right hand, lift it slightly to let me know you can hear me."

I lifted my finger.

"Very good. I am going to count down from 10. When I reach 1, you will be in a deep state of concentration."

This guy was actually trying to hypnotize me? Not today, fella. He counted down and then went into my behavior issues and gave me some trigger words to calm myself. By the time he counted back up, I was done with the nonsense but decided to give my parents their money's worth.

"Well, how do you feel?" he asked me.

"I guess I feel kind of refreshed. I don't know, maybe lighter. Not sure how to describe it," I said, acting happy. I stretched my arms and he seemed quite taken with himself.

"You did great." He put his big stupid hand on my shoulder and walked me back to my parents. They must have sensed the good news. My mom stood up and looked between me and the good doctor. I pretended to have my tail between my legs and smiled, thinking, "Yes Mommy, your puppy is housebroken."

I rolled my eyes to the invisible audience. Are these people this gullible?

On the way home, I sat in the back seat listening to my parents talk at me. My mom held up a book called something like, "How to Say No to Your Child". My mom was not going to read a book and especially not that book.

One afternoon, I was innocently laying on my bed reading "The World According to Garp". I had just finished the chapter where Garp dressed up like a woman so he could go to Jenny's memorial service, when there was a loud knock at my door.

"Go away," I said in a sweet but forceful voice. I was trying to be nice to everyone.

Another knock and the door was opened a crack and my mom stuck her head in.
"We have visitors," she said.

"I'm busy right now." I guess she didn't care because she opened the door further and came in followed by my father and both Brother Jon and Brother Henry. I sat up confused.

"May I?" Brother Jon motioned to the spot on my bed next to me. This was just too odd. I looked around hoping I hadn't left underwear in the middle of the floor.

"Your mom and dad are worried about you," he said. I looked at my mom who was looking down at the floor and looked at my dad who stood behind Brother Henry. "Would you mind if we prayed for you?"

Brother John had placed a bible on top of my dresser, next to a burned-out incense stick. He opened it to a page he had already marked. "Leave this open to this page to protect you," he said.

I wanted to scream at the top of my lungs, "Get the fuck out!" but I didn't. Instead I shrugged my shoulders, which was enough of an acknowledgement that they all leaned in and laid their hands on my head and shoulders.

I just closed my eyes hoping this was only a bad dream. It was reasonable that I could have a bad spirit inside me, I was a backslider.

"Jesus, we ask you for your patience and compassion. Please release our sister from the demons that live in her soul. Protect her from the evil spirits that have possessed her mind and body. I cast ye Satan out! In Jesus name, Amen"

"Amen."

"Amen."
"Amen."

Chapter 19

Dad had an opportunity to make some real money so he quit his job, cashed out his retirement account, and sold the house so he could start his own janitorial business. For the last year at West Coast he moved from being a grocery picker to becoming the night janitor where he learned how to use industrial type cleaning equipment.

"No one gets rich, working for other people," he said.

We said goodbye to our blue house on Fawcett and the best life we had so far. We just got a little too comfortable. I asked my parents if I could live with one of my friends. I didn't want to leave my friends. I would be in ninth grade at Stewart Junior High.

Brother and Sister Montoya and their two children, Larry and Nona, lived in the Nisqually Valley and were happy to take our family in. The only problem was there wasn't enough room for all of us, so Teresa and I moved into the single wide mobile home across the street from our parents and three younger sisters.

Nona was my age and Larry was a few years older. They were both heavily involved in the youth program at our church. They were originally from California and were missionaries. They were getting prepared for another missionary trip to Italy the following summer. When we moved, my dad traded Larry the 1968 Chevy Nova for a 35mm camera. I was devastated because my dad said I could have the car when I got my license. It had been sitting in front of our house for almost a year and I had been counting on driving it. At least he gave me the camera.

Teresa and I liked living in our own house across the street. It was like we were adults. We could cook and arrange everything like we wanted. There was a television there, but we were not supposed to watch it since it was against our religion.

The mobile home was owned by the neighbor, John, who was actually a real Nisqually Indian. He was a tall, good looking guy with long black hair that he pulled back in a ponytail. He dressed like a construction worker and drove an old fashioned pick-up truck with more rust than its original green.

We lived within walking distance of the river and the Nisqually reservation. The river became my happy place. I would walk along the river bank until I found a place to sit and watch the fast-moving water. It was so loud as it rushed by, you could barely hear your own thoughts, but it could soothe your soul. I had a favorite spot about halfway down the road that led to the Reservation. There was a large boulder with a flat top surrounded by bushes, but it had a clear view of the river. I liked the feeling of being invisible to the rest of the world.

If we had stayed in Tacoma, I would still be in junior high, but since we moved to the Nisqually Valley, we were now under the Thurston County school district, so I would be starting high school. The types of classes available were very different, and I chose photography (since I had a camera), graphic design, and pottery as my electives. Even though I was in a new school, I continued to do well in my required classes, math and English.

One of the required classes for ninth grade was Washington State History, where we were learning all about the indigenous people of the Pacific Northwest, including the Nisqually Indians. I was so fascinated that we lived so close, I checked out several books to learn more.

One evening, Teresa and I were attempting to make cookies, even though we didn't have all the ingredients, when we heard someone on the porch followed by a small knock. I opened the door and it was John, the Indian. It looked like he just got home from work. His clothes were dirty and I could smell fish guts mixed with man sweat.

"Your dad tells me you are interested in the Tribe," he said. I blushed, embarrassed that my dad said something to John about my obsession. I guess it was my fault since I was really excited and would tell the family interesting stories of life on the Nisqually people.

"Well...I...Well, we are reading about it in school." I said, hoping he wasn't offended.

"Would you like a tour of the hatchery?" he said, smiling.

"Sure," I said, "that would be great." I was actually really excited.

"I will pick you up Saturday morning at eight. Is that okay?"

"Yeah, sure," I said. "I would really like that." John went next door to his trailer, and as soon as the door shut, I ran across the street to tell my parents.

"John is taking me to the Reservation to see the hatchery," I said.

"That is great," my dad said. "If you get married, we can get Indian rights."

"I'm not getting married. I'm going on a tour."

"You never know," my dad said.

"Those Indian's like blonde hair," my mom said.

"I honestly don't think he is going to scalp me." I walked out shaking my head. My parents were totally serious. They would love to get rid of me.

Chapter 20

John had pulled up in front of our trailer a few minutes before eight and I was ready. I jumped up into the passenger side of the truck. It was fall and getting cold. I wished I had worn a thicker sweater. The reservation wasn't very far away but it was much larger than I thought. I had never been past the gates.

We started out with normal small talk—he told me about his family and I told him about living in the cabin like the early settlers. As soon as I felt comfortable, though, I started asking about his people and his personal experiences. I was fascinated and listened to every word.

His job was at the salmon hatchery, where there were giant tubs of salmon at different stages of maturity. This time of year, the salmon swam upstream, so I watched the salmon being plucked from a giant storage area. The workers were squeezing their bellies, forcing out eggs and putting the eggs into five-gallon buckets in which they were taken to be fertilized and would become baby salmon and eventually let back out into the Pacific to grow and replenish.

I helped him throw fish food into the different areas and watched the fish react as they came to the surface to eat. It was like a big tornado under water as the fish rushed to the pellets. John carried a clipboard and wrote notes as we went to different stations.

It was lunch time and he took me to his mom's house. She lived on the reservation in a moderate sized house. Most of the homes were white, single-story, and surrounded by chain link fences. There were no sidewalks and mostly dirt roads. His mom was short but not too short. She was pretty and looked young. She had made us sandwiches and John drank a beer. He offered me one but I settled for lemonade.

As we left the reservation, there were some places with junk cars without wheels, forgotten laundry that barely held on to clothes lines, and dirty faced children playing in the streets. We left a long white dust trail as we turned to the paved road.

Overall, I had a great day. John was funny and told me jokes I had never heard before. I tried to remember them so I could tell my sisters. He was a handsome guy, but definitely too old for me.

I wondered if he ever wore his hair in two braids like all the pictures I'd ever seen of Indians. No one I met that day really looked like the pictures of Indians from the books I had read, maybe because they wore normal clothes and spoke normal English. They were just normal people.

"I had a great time today," he said.

"Me too." I opened the door to get out. The truck was still running even though we were parked between the two trailers. My foot found the side step and suddenly he was at my door reaching to help me down. When both feet were safely on the ground, he leaned into me and his mouth was now on my mouth. He was kissing me and I wasn't sure what to do, so I kissed back. His kiss was sloppy and I wasn't into it at all. I just wanted it to stop.

"Is something wrong?" he asked.

"I have to go," I said. His hands were wrapped around me now, cupping my butt and pulling me into him.

"I'm only 15," I said.

"I know, your dad told me."

"I don't think it's legal."

"Who is going to tell?" He laughed but let go and stepped back. "Do you know what a cock tease is, little girl?" I shook my head no. "Well I do!" He didn't go into his trailer but got back into his truck and drove off.

It had been such a good day and I couldn't understand what had just happened or what I might have done to make John think I wanted to be his girlfriend—unless my dad had arranged a marriage without me knowing. I really didn't understand men.

Chapter 21

John went out of his way to avoid me, which was good for me but made living next door in his trailer awkward, so it was a relief when we finally moved a few miles away into a brand-new doublewide in a small mobile home park. Teresa and I shared a room but we didn't mind. She liked to have everything neat and I was a slob, but she cleaned our room so our dad didn't yell at me. The way I cleaned was to shove everything under my bed.

We still got to go to the same school where I made some non-Pentecostal friends. My ceramics class was really fun. I got to make a bowl on the wheel and an ashtray by rolling up the clay and shaping it. Most of the class manufactured bongs. I think my teacher was a hippy and a pot head, because he really didn't care that the drying racks were full of a variety of bongs. I wanted to make a bong but knew my mom would throw it away, so I made a coffee mug for my mom as a Christmas present.

My favorite class was graphic arts. Ever since that office lady let me help her with the mimeograph, I was fascinated with these machines. I knew this was my future. The teachers and students were the "cool" people. They were also the artistic type of pot smokers that listened to KZOK on the radio during class.

I was a kid that didn't fit into one group. I loved hanging with the pot heads who had cool cars, the band geeks, and the smart kids in student government. I didn't have one personality, I easily fit in with whoever I was with at the time. I did get most of my student government friends high for the first time.

My typical Saturday could include marching in a parade playing the flute or oboe in the morning and going to a kegger that night. Jason was my friend from band who also liked to get high and Karen was in my ceramics class. I first met Karen in class. She let me eat lunch with her and introduced me to some of her friends.

Parties where usually out in the middle of the woods or at some out of the way cabin. Boys had to pay a couple bucks for their red cup, but most of the time girls were free.

One of these parties was out in the middle of nowhere. It was an abandoned house with a broken fence. There was some furniture but it was old and smelled like mold. Two boys stood at the front door collecting $5 a piece for the beer. There were so many kids stuffed into the living room, where the keg stood, you could barely move.

My friends and I found a bedroom where we passed around a joint.

"Watch this," Jason said. He was one of the "cool kids" because he played the drums. Jason picked up a small calico kitten and held it close to his face.

"Oh, my God," Karen said. "Knock it off." She reached out to take the kitten from Jason but he moved too fast and attempted to blow the smoke in the kitten's face again. The kitten didn't seem high and the smoke just seemed to make it sneeze.

All of a sudden there was a loud commotion in the living room, Jason threw the kitten across the bed and we all went out to see what was going on. There was a fight between two boys who were older, maybe even out of school. They were punching and hitting until one of them fell to the ground. I am not sure how I ended up so close to the action, but the next thing I knew, the boy with the advantage moved back enough that he had room and, in slow motion, his leg went back and then moved forward, kicking the boy on the ground with a huge brown work boot. The impact was dead on and above the noise of the crowd that surrounded me I heard a hollow thump, like a watermelon dropped to the ground. The room stopped—silent—and there was blood. The kicking boy ran and so did everyone else.

"We need to get out of here," Karen said and I followed her out the back door where we ran with everyone else. I didn't see anyone help the boy on the ground. He just laid there. I couldn't get the hollow sound out of my head.

The next week at school, I heard the boy had died. I had witnessed a murder, but not one person talked and the other boy was never arrested, as far as I knew. I couldn't say anything because I would be in so much trouble if my parents found out that I had been to a party.

David Coleman was in my math class. He was super nice and I really liked him. He was not the boyfriend type, but more like a best friend. Some of the kids thought he was odd because he carried around a bible along with his school books.

To keep the peace at home, I had agreed to go to church on Sundays, so I decided to invite David to come to church with me. I figured it would be more tolerable with a friend.

"I don't have a ride," he said.

"My dad will give you a ride," I said. I knew my dad would be more than happy to give someone a ride to church.

"I just want to warn you, they speak Spanish and get a little crazy," I said. David smiled. Like many kids that lived around there, his dad was in the army. His mom was Korean and his dad was white. Whenever I went to his house, it smelled like garlic. You couldn't help stopping, right when you walked in the door, and taking a deep breath with your nose, filling your whole body with the magical aroma.

David really liked our church and started even going to youth group. He even became a member of our carpool. Larry drove Nona, me, and now David to school every day in a small green Volkswagen. He didn't have the Nova running yet. Larry and David sat in the front and Nona and I squeezed into the back.

One foggy morning, on the way to school, we were hit by a cement truck that had run the light and smashed right into us. The car rolled over and over like a ball that had been kicked down the street. When it finally settled, I remember wondering if I was dead. I couldn't really move. None of us wore seatbelts and we were all tangled up. I was laying on Nona. One by one, we all somehow got out of the smashed-up vehicle. It was a miracle that none of us was seriously hurt. Nona had to wear a neck brace for a few weeks and I think Larry had crutches for a little while so, we all had to take the bus.

The buses here were yellow school buses, not like the city buses we took when we lived in Tacoma. It wasn't bad taking the bus because I made new friends in my neighborhood. One friend, Carol, didn't live in our mobile home park but across the street in a nice single-story brick house. Her father was a retired Army Sergeant who met her mother when he was stationed in Germany.

Carol was a year older but didn't mind hanging out with me. That summer she got her own car and was able to get a job at the Capital Mall. I wanted to get a job, too, but I wasn't old enough. She worked at the Great Hot Dog Experience, where you could get a regular hot dog or a German sausage and fix it up with any kind of condiments—some you couldn't even imagine. They even had black olives and diced tomatoes. Sometimes, I would go with Carol to the mall. She would work and I would walk around. I got to know a lot of the other kids working, and I really wanted to get a job, so I filled out a job application at Orange Julius and The Great Hot Dog Experience. I lied about my age and was interviewed by both managers. I decided to take the Hot Dog job since I didn't really have a way to get to work and could ride with Carol.

My job lasted less than two weeks because somehow the manager found out that I wasn't sixteen yet. I was disappointed because there weren't a lot of opportunities in the area to make money.

Chapter 22

Maybe it was our near-death experience in the car wreck or just pure devotion that drove David to get baptized at the church, so I reluctantly went to the Friday night service even though I had a really bad side ache. I was the one who got him into the church, so I figured it was the least I could do.

The church was surprisingly full. I hadn't been to a Friday night in a very long time. Both David's parents and his sister were there. It was quite an event.

"Nice to see you here tonight," brother Gonzalas said to me.

"I wanted to see David get baptized," I said.

"The Lord works through certain people and I believe you are one of those people," he said, smiling, "you just don't know it yet."

At that, I laughed out loud. He didn't get mad—just stood there smiling. I actually liked Jon Gonzalas. I would probably have liked him more if he hadn't influenced my parents so much, but if not for him, who knows what might have happened. I always wondered if it was better having ultra-religious parents or drunkards.

"What are you up to this summer?" he asked.

"Nothing," I said disappointedly. I really wished I had a job.

"Have you ever been to California?"

"No."

"Would you like to go with Jessica, the boys and me to California next week?" I took a step back and tried to clear my head. Did he just ask me to go to California? How awkward would it be?

"I guess so," I said. Since I didn't have a job, I figured 'what the heck'.

I sat in the back seat with the boys and I taught them how to play slug bug and the alphabet game. They were the same age as Lisa and Josette, and they liked me, so the time went by pretty fast. Sitting so long gave me a side ache. No matter how I stretched around, I couldn't get it to stop hurting. Sister Gonzalas gave me aspirin, which seemed to help. We drove all night and finally reached Los Angeles the next day. We were staying with Brother Gonzalas's sister.

I absolutely loved California. It was sunny and warm. I decided this was where I was going to live when I grew up.

Brother Gonzalas had a niece and nephew my age. John was the boy's name, probably named after his uncle. He was a Beatles super-fan. Every wall in his room was plastered with posters, album covers and miscellaneous Beatles memorabilia. He even had a Beatles hairstyle. The girl's name was Juanita and she looked identical to her brother except she wore her dark brown hair pulled back into a pony tail. She was more into sports and had medals and awards hanging all over the walls in her room. I was surprised both kid's bedrooms were so neat and tidy, everything in its place.

Brother Gonzalas was so different than I had seen at church. He was just a normal guy around his family. He hardly ever talked about God. He even gave me money so I could go to Six Flags with his niece.

I had never been to anything like Six Flags. It was crowded with kids my age. You could go on any of the rides you wanted to, but Juanita just wanted to hang out with her friends. We found four girls who she called her family.

"What's with the gringa?" one of the girls said. I knew enough Spanish to know that "gringa" meant "white girl".

"She is not a gringa," Juanita said. "She is from Seattle and she is Mexican."

The girls were not very friendly and they argued in Spanish. I didn't understand much except that I should keep my mouth shut. Later, Juanita told me the girls were in a gang and that the rule is that you have to go through initiation to hang out with them, but since I was only staying a week, I didn't have to.

"What is the initiation?" I asked, not that I had any interest in being in a gang. I was just curious.

"The members form a circle around the prospect and hit and kick as much as they can for at least five minutes."

"Oh shit!"

"Yeah."

The week went by pretty fast, and I enjoyed hanging out with Juanita. She was surprised that I smoked pot since her uncle was my pastor. I explained that I was the rebel of the family.

"I'm the black sheep," I said. "Well, actually I guess I am the white sheep." We both laughed.

The trip home was miserable. My side ache was getting worse and I tried to push in with my fist but it just wouldn't go away. When I got home, I suffered in silence so I wouldn't have to go to the doctor. My mother loved to run to the hospital for any little thing. I hated hospitals and doctors.

I felt like I was going to throw up so I ran to the bathroom and leaned over the toilet. I don't remember what happened after that but, apparently, Teresa had found me passed out, laying on the bathroom floor curled up in a ball.

I barely remember the ambulance ride to the hospital or the hospital staff that examined me when we got there. It was more like a dream or an out of body experience where I just looked down at myself. The last thing I remember is a mask being placed over my mouth and nose and the funny smell of rubber.

The next thing I remember is waking up in a hospital bed and my mom sitting on a chair next to the bed with a worried look on her face.

"You are a lucky girl," said a grey-haired man who was most likely the doctor. He moved my gown and pushed around on my stomach with his big cold hands. "You had a cyst the size of a grapefruit just about to burst. If you hadn't come in when you did, we wouldn't be talking right now." I blinked in acknowledgement because really, he was doing all the talking.

When he left, I asked my mom what happened.

"They thought it was that your appendix had burst, but it was your right ovary. They took the appendix since they were already there. Do you know what an ovary is?" I rolled my eyes like "of course I do," but wasn't exactly sure. Our religion didn't allow us to participate in sex education.

"It's the place in a woman's body where the eggs are stored. Every month one of the eggs moves into the uterus to get fertilized. If there is no fertilization, it washes away. That is why you have a period. The doctor said it may be hard for you to get pregnant when you are older with only one ovary."

"Thank God, I don't want any kids," I said.

"Well, you might change your mind. He wanted to take the other ovary but I said no."

I wished I had a book but I was just too tired. I needed words to fill my brain.

"Can you read to me?" I asked my mother. She went out and got a Readers Digest from the waiting room and started reading. I fell asleep.

1944: Nelda Mae (Age 18)

Clara held Nelda's hand while she had another contraction. She wasn't handling the labor very well and wanted some gas to knock her out but they were in the military hospital where the doctors didn't believe in gas.

"Where is Elmer," Nelda asked her mother between her wails.

"He's in the waiting room," her mother said calmly.

"Can you ask him to come back here?"

"They won't let him. He is not the father."

"I need to see him." She started crying and, as usual, her mother acquiesced to her daughters wishes, but the hospital refused.

Nelda met her husband George in the neighborhood, but they lived on opposite sides of town. George worked for his father, who had a successful wood floor installation company. He was a tall red head with bright blue eyes and money in his pocket. George had joined the army, so the couple decided to get married.

George was stationed overseas when Nelda met Elmer, also an army man, stationed in Seattle as part of a security force. She was lonely and Elmer reminded her of Clark Gable. He knew she was married but couldn't resist the sassy young girl.

The baby girl finally made it into the world and Elmer was allowed to see Nelda. Nelda handed him the baby, asking "What should we name her?"

"I would like to name her after my mother, Bernice Lucille."

George received two telegrams that day, one congratulating him on the birth of a baby girl and the other from his wife, asking for a divorce. George refused to divorce Nelda and she couldn't force it because he was active military. She would have to wait until he came home.

Nelda didn't like to be told no, so she enlisted George's father, who just lived a few miles away. He agreed to go to court with her and deny the child was his son's. The judge didn't buy it and George remained the father on the birth certificate.

X

1979: Charisse (Age 16)

Chapter 23

We never got to go to the Puyallup Fair even though we got free tickets at school every September. Either we couldn't afford it or my parents didn't have time. Today was no different—we drove right past the giant cow and up the hill to 1818 South Meridian to attend a special church service at the World of Pentecost. It was almost 2 pm and it looked like the fair traffic was out of control, but as soon as we got through a few blocks, there was even more traffic going into the parking lot of the huge church.

We walked into a huge auditorium where we were greeted on both sides by two men in expensive looking suits, both with identical haircuts but one much older than the other. The men introduced themselves to our group and led us to one of the only rows still available in the back of the filled church. The place was bustling with women like us, dressed in dresses, hair either piled on top or flowing long, down past their waists, the only difference was that the women at this church did not wear veils so our small group stood out.

The stage extended across the front, covered wall to wall with deep royal purple carpet that matched the soft upholstery of the pews, a lot more comfortable than the solid wood benches at our small church. Two giant screens hung on each side of the stage, lit up with a welcoming message and picture of the visiting pastor from California, the reason we were visiting this church. Alex and Roberta Melendez knew the visiting pastor and convinced my parents that he would deliver a powerful message.

Under the left screen was a small group of instruments including a full drum set, an electric guitar, a bass, and a keyboard, with several microphones strategically placed in front of the ensemble. Soon, from both sides of the stage, people walked from the back and took their places.

Music took over the room and quieted the chatter. Everyone stood facing the front. There was a balcony that ended directly above my head so it was impossible to see the people, but I could hear their voices as they started singing along with the words that appeared on both screens. Watching the singers and band in front, I felt like I was at a professional performance, only with audience participation.

The singing went on for at least a half hour, I was too tired and wanted to sit down but didn't want to attract any attention to myself, so I stood. It was a relief when a tall blonde man, who looked more like a movie star than a pastor, took his place in front of a clear glass podium.

Pastor Gene Larsen, a tall blonde Norwegian with sharp features, welcomed the parishioners as well as the visitors motioning to our small group in the back rows. The visiting pastor from California was a short dark Hispanic man who had such a booming voice he hardly needed a microphone. He frequently pulled a handkerchief out of his pocket to wipe the sweat from his forehead and the back of his neck and then returned it to the same pocket he took it from.

By the end of the service, women and men were crying, some in front on their knees dedicating their lives to god, while I sat watching the commotion and getting impatient to get out of this church.

After the service, Pastor Gene Larson with his blonde Ken doll hair and several of his bookend deacons, came to greet the strangers with veil-covered wives and children.

"Welcome to The World of Pentecost," he said with his perfectly straight white TV smile. The bookends stood close behind almost like a personal security detail. "Where are you visiting from?"

My father spoke for the small group, "Tacoma, Apostolic Assembly."

"Brother Gonzalas's church," he said, still smiling, and his blue eyes moved from person to person, acknowledging or sizing each of us up. We were all surprised that he knew about our small church. "I would like to invite you to stay and socialize with us. There are refreshments in the foyer. Please..." He motioned out towards the back of the church where several doors led to the large space where many of the parishioners had gathered and were chit chatting in small groups.

Over the next several weeks, my parents and the Melendez's attended services and bible studies with the Pentecostals. By the third week we were no longer going to the Apostolic Assembly and were now fulltime members of the World of Pentecost.

"How did you decide to switch to Brother Larsen's church?" I asked my mom, even though I should have been asking my dad because, ultimately, it was always his decision.

"He recognized the veils as Apostolic," she said. "The doctrine they were preaching at the Apostolic Assembly was not of God. It was the doctrine of a faith healer William M. Branham who broke with traditional Pentecostal values. He said that Jon Gonzalas was a well-known Branhamite."

"So what," I said. "What's the big difference?"

"It's how you interpret the bible." She was beginning to get flustered.

"What's the main difference?" I asked.

"If you go to church more often, you could see." She was done.

"What I see is just more bull-shit wrapped in a prettier package." I said it so she couldn't hear me, but I was just glad we were Branhamites instead of Mennonites.

The best and worst part of leaving the Apostolic Assembly behind was that we didn't have to wear veils to church, but that meant the end of my small manufacturing business.

Of course, I didn't let it go, because I really liked to be right. I had to ask, "Why don't we have to wear veils to church, according to the bible in I Corinthians?"

"The bible says, a woman's hair is her glory given to her for a covering," my mom said.

So basically, the same chapter but a few verses difference was the reason we were required to wear veils and NOT to wear veils. Specifically, my mom stopped wearing a veil because a few sentences past the verse that convinced her to wear a veil, convinced her that long hair was good enough. I Corinthians 11:15 "But if a woman has long hair, it is a glory to her: for her hair is given her for a covering".

The family easily assimilated into the giant church. My mom, Josette and Angelique all joined the music programs, my dad joined the men's groups and started wearing suits matching the other men. Almost every evening, there was something church related going on. I wasn't interested and had my own life to live, which did not include joining a cult, although I did attend church and a few youth activities, mostly as a bargaining chip to get something out of my parents.

One of the things we learned at The World of Pentecost was that the end of the world was near. We watched movies and listened to the horrors that would befall us if we weren't right with God and were left behind. Left behind meant all the godly people who lived right would be scooped up by God, leaving all the sinners behind to endure floods, fire and terrible famine. We would have sores all over our bodies and suffer terrible pain. Some of these guys were so convincing, I would practically run to the front of the church asking for forgiveness, begging God to give me another chance. Usually, I couldn't keep my promises more than a week.

I wasn't the only one in the church that fell for the end of the world threat. Most of the people in the church were true believers. Many of the girls were in such a hurry to live, they didn't even finish high school before they got married. It was a socially acceptable practice for your kid to be married at 16 as long as the boy was from the church.

I think word got out in town because we had quite a few 18- and 19-year-old boys converted into the Pentecostal religion so they could have access to all these willing virgins. Even though I didn't buy most of the bullshit, I couldn't help getting caught up in the mania. What if it was true? What if the world was going to end in 2 years or even 5 years. I felt a little rushed to get married and have kids.

One of the older guys at church asked me out on a date. I wasn't allowed to date, but of course my dad said okay because it was a guy from church. Sherman was a tall boy with dark black hair. He was a little shy, overweight but taller than me and I liked that. This was my first "real" date and I wasn't really sure how to act. He was a church boy, so we wouldn't be drinking. He came to the front door, greeted my parents and even opened the car door for me. Usually I was pretty confident around church people because I didn't care what they thought. I wanted everyone to know I was not one of them, but this was different. I was feeling a bit shaky, nervous.

He took me to the Puyallup Fair, which was another first. I had never been, and all the sights and sounds were overwhelming. We went on rides and ate a lot of different foods. He even won me a huge stuffed bear. I had never had so much fun in my whole life, especially with a boy. Maybe he would be the one I would marry someday. I was overwhelmed in the excitement of it all.

We parked about a block away from my house so we could talk a while before I went in. He told me about his family and his job. He had his own house and was ready to settle down. I told him about school and my sisters. He leaned over and kissed me. It was very sweet and soft. I liked it a lot.

"I need to ask you something," he said.

"Okay," I said.

"Will you marry me?" He had both my hands in his hands, staring me right in the eye. I didn't even really know this guy. We had talked a few times at church. I knew he had a crush on me, but marriage? He saw the shock on my face, so he started to kiss me again. Instead of answering, I kept kissing. Maybe he would give me hickies so my dad would hate him.

"Will you marry me?" he whispered in my ear. I guess he really wanted an answer. What I should have said was, "Can I answer that tomorrow?" or "Can we at least go on one more date?" But instead, I felt bad.

"Okay, sure," I said, because I didn't want to hurt his feelings.

"I will bring you a ring tomorrow, okay?" He sat back, excited.

"Okay," I said. I stared at his face, trying to memorize it since I had never really looked at him that way. I tried to picture our wedding. He was tall enough, I could wear heels. I had a lot to think about.

"I knew you were the one, the first time I saw you," he said excitedly.

I couldn't even remember the first time I saw him. "I need to go home now," I said, looking at my watch, but it was too dark to see what time it really was. He started up the car and drove me down the block to my house. He got out of the car and ran to my side to let me out. My heart was racing and I was speechless. He kissed me again. He walked me all the way to the front door. He was a very polite young man. My mom would like him.

"I'll be here as soon as I can tomorrow morning sometime, okay?" He looked longingly in my eyes and I shook my head with a smile on my face to disguise my real feelings.

I walked in the door and sat down right at the threshold so I wouldn't fall down. I was getting married. "I can't get married… I'm too young." I said out loud. How am I going to get out of this? If he brought me the ring, I would be stuck. It might be fun to be married and it would get me out of this house, but I didn't really love this guy. I wondered if I would learn to love him like people who had arranged marriages do.

It was late but I couldn't sleep so I knocked on my parent's bedroom door.

"Are you guys awake? I have a huge problem," I said through the closed door.

"Come in, what's the problem?" my dad asked. Both my parents were now sitting up.

"Sherman asked me to marry him," I just blurted out.

"What did you say?" my mom asked.

"Yes."

"Well he seems like a nice boy," my mom said. I knew she liked him. He told her she had the most beautiful eyes. She could never resist a compliment.

"I don't want to get married."

"Then why did you say yes?" she asked.

"I don't know. I felt bad if I said no." I looked at my dad. "You have to talk to him and tell him I am not allowed to get married. Just say I'm too young."

"Okay," my dad said, like no big deal.

"He is bringing me an engagement ring tomorrow, so you have to be home."

The next day, Sherman came to the door, but I stayed in my room while my dad talked to him. I did write him a letter trying to let him down easy. I didn't want him to feel bad or commit suicide.

He never talked to me again and never came back to church. I wondered if I got a strike against me from God for that one.

Chapter 24

The janitorial business ended up being a great success. Dad started his business by going to work with a bucket and squeegee. He would offer to wash potential clients' windows for free. The ones impressed would let him bid on their cleaning contracts. Once he built up a regular client schedule, he hired more people and bid on the janitorial services at Fort Lewis Army Base and McCord Airforce Base. He also had Ross stores up and down the West Coast and a variety of other small businesses, including cleaning newly constructed apartment buildings.

All of us girls worked for our dad at one time or another. There is something about cleaning that is very satisfying, walking into a business trashed from the day's customers, and a few hours later seeing it in perfect order. Things seemed to be improving. We finally had enough money for a real house back in Tacoma.

My dad made a deal with a contractor to build a dream house. We each picked out colors for the walls and carpet for our room. The house was almost complete when the contractor disappeared. At the same time he disappeared, the house was robbed. They took everything, including all the appliances, rolls of carpet that hadn't been installed, even the toilets. The rumor was that he took off with several projects' money and was now living comfortably somewhere in Mexico.

Our new house was finally finished in spite of the harassment from the unpaid contractors. It was a split entry house with a daylight basement. As you walked in the door, you stood on a small landing. If you went up about five steps you could walk straight into the kitchen or turn right into the large living room with a giant glass window facing the street. I slept downstairs, where we had converted the rec room into my bedroom. I actually had a sliding glass door in my room—which would come in handy for sneaking out at night.

The only problem was that the house was outside the school district we were in before the move to Nisqually, but since Tacoma was an open district, Teresa and I were able to go back to school with our old friends on the South side.

The first day of school was a little nerve-racking since I had to take the city bus across town and wasn't sure what stop I needed to get off at 38th street. I missed my stop so I had to walk a few extra blocks. I hated being late and felt like crying but was relieved when I reached the office and it was full of students waiting for their schedules. It was almost second period when I finally got my schedule. I just hoped I could find my classes. It looked like I only had one class on the second floor and one in the basement.

Walking down the hall, I was looking at the classroom doors and soon figured out the numbering. I realized I was on the opposite side of the school from my second-period class, so I quickly turned around and walked right into a small group of letter-jacket-clad football players. I moved to the side to let them pass when the largest of them broke off and started following me. I could tell he was following me but didn't want to acknowledge him, so I stopped, looking down, pretending to study my class schedule.

"What's your name?" he said in a deep voice. I turned around to face him. He was well over 6 feet tall, with blond, feathered hair that curled at his big shoulders. He was like a Greek god, and I could hardly speak.

"Charisse Orona," I said softly. My eyes felt like they were bulging out of my head, and I couldn't blink. I knew from experience that anything that came out of my mouth at this point wouldn't make sense or would make me sound stupid. I was usually a good communicator—just not with foxy guys.

"My Shiroma!" he said, smiling his amazing smile. He started humming the tune to the *Knacks* song before he asked, "Are you going to the game?" I had no idea what game he was referring to but nodded and smiled anyway.

"Cool," he said as he turned and jogged to the end of the hall where the rest of his gang waited. I watched as they turned down the front hall. I was in shock. I definitely did not have the self-esteem necessary to pursue this guy, way out of my league.

I went to the game but sat with my friends as part of the band, in which I was the only oboe player. I was glad we didn't have uniforms issued yet and could wear whatever we wanted. I wore the tightest jeans I owned, which really showed off my butt. It didn't take long before Mr. Perfect spotted me in the stands and waved. I was shocked but excited and a little embarrassed that I was in the band.

Janet leaned over to me. "Oh shit. Did Ray just wave at you?"

"I think so," I said, red faced.

"Just be careful, he has a reputation. That is his twin brother, David." She pointed to our quarterback. The two boys did not look like twins. Ray was twice the size of his brother. He was definitely the cutest one.

"I'm not interested in him," I said. "I didn't even know his name before tonight."

Janet rolled her eyes. "He is definitely fine, but he is a senior."

"Yes, he is," I agreed.

For the next few weeks, anytime I saw Ray in the hall, he broke off from his group and came over to me, put his arm around me and sang lyrics to the song My Shiroma. He gave me his phone number and told me to call him. I wasted no time and called him that night and for the next few nights. I sat under the kitchen table, stretching the phone cord as far as it would stretch, trying to maintain some privacy. If I wasn't talking to Ray, I was talking to one of my friends. My dad said I was going to get "cauliflower ear".

It was a few days before Halloween when Ray was telling me about a Halloween party he was having at his house. He didn't really invite me, but I figured I was invited.

"Why don't you come over tonight and I will show you the decorations," he said. I said okay and he told me where he lived. I was going to have to take the bus but I didn't care.

I knocked at the door and Ray was right there to greet me. He pulled me in and without any warning kissed me right on the mouth. It was hard and rough and I was not really ready for it, so I just shook it off. He took me by the hand and led me down the stairs where there were two other boys and Ray's brother sitting in beanbags and on the couch, each of them sat next to a girl. I only recognized one of the girls from my homeroom. The whole basement was decorated with spider webs, pumpkins and witches. The record player was playing Pink Floyd's Dark Side of the Moon. Ray sat on a beanbag and pulled me onto his lap. He grabbed my breasts and cupped them in his hands as he leaned in for another kiss. He put his tongue in and out quickly like he was licking an ice cream. Everyone else was also making out. I tried to enjoy myself, focusing on the fact that this was one of the most popular boys in the school. I imagined myself by his side at all the dances, being the envy of all the popular girls. I actually would be part of their click.

Ray stood and pulled me to him, leading me down the hall into his bedroom where he laid me on his bed and got on top of me. I could barely breathe as he put his hand up my shirt and roughly pinched my nipple. It hurt so bad I almost let a tear fall from my eye. He then found the top button of my pants and unbuttoned it. I gently grabbed his hand and moved it away but he persisted. I started to panic and wiggled out from under him.

"What's the matter?" he said, surprised as I sat up and re-buttoned my pants.

"I am on my period," I said, even though I wasn't. I was still a virgin. I really wanted to be with Ray, but it wasn't like I imagined. He was supposed to be my Prince Charming—now I just needed to get out of there.

"Okay. Fine," he said, sounding irritated, and I felt ashamed. As soon as I got out of the house, I started to cry and continued to cry until I got to my house. It was almost 8 o'clock when I finally got enough nerve to call Ray.

"I just wanted to say goodnight," I said, trying to sound normal, but I was sad.

"Here is the deal. I don't want you to call me anymore. If I want to talk to you, I will call you." The phone clicked dead. I sat under the kitchen table where I had taken the phone for some privacy. I couldn't move. I felt like someone just punched me in the stomach. I couldn't swallow. I was a fool. I couldn't move. How was I going to show my face at school? I wished I knew where my real dad lived so I could move in with him.

"Jesus Fucking Christ," I said aloud to the phone I still had in my hand. I just got dumped and we never even went out on a real date. I cried all night, swearing I would never let a guy break my heart again. The next time I saw Ray, he had his arm around another sophomore in the hall just as he had me only a few days before. I guess this was how he caught his victims. I was no more than an "almost" notch on his bedpost.

"Can I go to Mt. Tahoma?" I asked my mom. Mt. Tahoma was the closest school to us and I was pretty sure I had some friends that went there.

"Sure. If you want," my mom said. My parents really didn't care if we went to school or not. I ended up getting over it and stayed at Lincoln.

Since Lincoln didn't have graphic arts, I was put into a drafting class. I didn't even know what drafting was, so I thought I would have to transfer out, but when I showed up the first day, I walked in and saw that every desk in the whole classroom was occupied by a boy, not one girl. "I think I found Heaven," I said to myself in a whisper.

Even though it was all the testosterone that made me stay enrolled in the class, it was drafting itself that became my obsession. I loved the control of drawing perfect angles and straight t-squared lines with varying thickness, showing exploded machines exposing every gear and bolt, labeling each piece with perfectly vertical 1/8th all capital lettering. I spent hours and days bent over my drafting board, creating the perfect house that I swore I would build one day.

In metal shop, I wasn't expected to do much since I was a girl—any effort I put out was like a miracle. We made sand molds and poured liquid metal into them and came back the next day to release the project and clean it up with a Dremel tool and sandpaper.

One day, I was in the welding booth with my hood on, trying to perfect stick welding, when someone came up behind me and grabbed my ass. I screamed in shock and the teacher ran over, thinking I had an accident with the welding machine or maybe burned myself. When I told him what happened, he got red faced and gave me an "A" without my having to finish any of my welds. I was happy for the "A" but never got to TIG weld.

I was involved in lots of school activities. During my junior year, I was a JV cheerleader and my dad showed up for a basketball game to watch me perform. My parents had never come to any of my activities, so I was a little surprised and nervous. I always imagined being one of those kids whose parents participated, but my dad was always working and my mom never had a way to get anywhere since she didn't want to drive. They didn't care one way or another if I participated in school activities, but I had to pay whatever the cost was by myself. Usually it wasn't a lot of money, but cheerleading was very expensive. One uniform cost $300. I would have to get a real job so I could afford it. Being a cheerleader was not all I hoped it would be. I wouldn't do it next year.

Chapter 25

My first "real" job was as a waitress at Mr. Steak. It was my first glimpse into adulthood. Most of the people I worked with were in their 20s and 30s. I showed up for training with two other girls. I took home a menu and memorized what I could and then practiced taking orders from my sisters.

"How would you like your steak cooked… baked potatoes, mashed potatoes, or rice pilaf…soup or salad?" I had no idea what rice pilaf was!

The second day I showed up in my brown and orange polyester uniform. Rachel, the trainer and also the owner's wife, said," I guess you don't want to make any money?" I was confused. Of course, I wanted to make money. She pointed at my hem, "Shorten your skirt."

I loved being a waitress and I would work whenever they asked. I did double shifts and would even fill in as a hostess if needed. The customers loved me and the owners always sat in my section, which I felt was a compliment, even though they seldom tipped me. I was willing to give up my Friday and Saturday nights hanging out with my friends for the roll of cash I had at the end of the night. I could easily make $100 on a good night. I had never had this much money in my whole life.

"Good job tonight," Michael said. He was our manager and really hadn't said much to me before. He was 25 years old and very handsome. He had dark brown hair and blue eyes like Clark Brandon, one of the teen idol posters I had hanging on my bedroom wall. The only negative was he was a little bit shorter than me. I really liked taller guys.

"Thank you," I said, wiping down the table with the vinegar smelling cloth that had been white earlier in the shift. Most of the girls hated closing but I liked it because of how quiet it was when there were just one or two tables left. I didn't even mind crawling under the tables and sweeping out crumbs from under the bench seats so we could vacuum.

"Would you like to go to a party?" Michael asked.

"Sure," I said. I knew the crew always got together after work, but I was only a teenager so no one ever invited me. I finished up while Michael waited for me. I followed him, driving the family station wagon, and parked as close as I could to the small house crowded with people. There were cars and people everywhere. I recognized most of them, but they looked so different in their street clothes. I was used to seeing the cooks in their whites and all the girls in the same uniform I was currently wearing.

"I should have gone home and changed," I said as I looked around. It felt so awkward being around these people. I could smell the greasy kitchen smell in my hair. I felt out of place.

"You look great," Michael said as he put his arm around me and led me into the chaos. We made it through the crowd to the kitchen and Michael made me a drink called a Bloody Jesus. I never heard of such a thing and I didn't really want to try it but was desperate to fit in. I drank it. It was just purple grape juice and Vodka, a lot of vodka. Michael and I sat together on the couch. He kept his arm around me or touched my leg. I saw Christa, across the room, roll her eyes at us. She was one of the first waitresses they hired when Mr. Steak opened and was good friends with the owners. I was pretty sure she was sleeping with the husband because, whenever his wife wasn't there, she would go in the office with him and they would close the door.

The crowd thinned as people started leaving. I felt like I should go home but Michael convinced me to stay. He kissed me and I kissed him back. His lips were soft and experienced. He had his hands all over my body and I almost forgot where I was. I wished I wasn't so drunk. It wasn't long before he was on top of me with my skirt up and my panties down. He pushed a few times and got all the way in.

"Oh, my God," he said in a satisfied whisper. "You were a virgin." He pushed a few more times and I wanted to cry from the pain. He finished and rolled off me. I didn't know what to do but found my panties and put them on. He kissed me lightly on the forehead and fell asleep. I couldn't sleep and just wanted to get home. Was I pregnant? Was Michael my boyfriend? Did anyone see what happened? No one was around and I carefully got up and walked out the door.

When I got home, I couldn't take a shower because I would wake up my parents and it was after 2 am, but I tried to wipe off the remnants of the evening. My mind was racing and I couldn't sleep. I didn't pray very often, but that night I made a deal with God.

"Please God, I promise never to do this again if you can just make sure I'm not pregnant. Amen."

Michael was at work Wednesday night, which was the first time I had seen him since our "get together". I was embarrassed and didn't know how to act, so I avoided him as much as one can avoid their manager. He acted the same, as if nothing ever happened, so I slowly evolved into the same stance and by the end of the night everything was back to normal—except I had to live with the fact I had slept with my manager.

I walked into the staging area of the kitchen where Christa was standing eating the fried shrimp off a customer's plate she had cleared. "Can't let perfectly good shrimp go to waste." It totally grossed me out.

"You know he's married, right?"

"Who?" I asked, feeling my face turn flush. She rolled her eyes and walked away.

XI

1980: Charisse (Age 17)

Chapter 26

Mr. Ochs was my guidance counselor. He was an average, middle-aged man who was prematurely grey, probably from working at a high school in the worst part of town. I had met with him several times, arranging to take my SATs, and I also had some interest in the military so I had taken the ASVAB test. He was always smiling when I walked in.

"Have you ever thought about working at a shipyard?" he asked.

"I never even heard of that kind of job, "I said. "What would I do?"

"There is a work study program at Puget Sound Naval Shipyard, where you work during the summer of your junior year and then half your senior year and get full credits for school," he explained.

"Do I get paid?"

"Yes, of course. It's a great program. Honestly, I think it's a perfect fit."

"I will think about it," I said.

"Fill this out." He handed me a thick packet of paperwork.

"Jeez, that's a lot of paperwork," I said.

"It's the government."

I wasn't sure I wanted to give up being a waitress. The tips were incredible. Also, if I worked full time instead of going to school, I would have to withdraw from the race for Class Treasurer. I had already hung all the posters. I took the paperwork home anyway and filled it out, just in case.

I told my parents about the program, since I had to have them fill out some of the forms. I knew they wouldn't do it, so I filled it all out for them and all they needed to do was sign.

"You actually want to work at a factory?" my dad said. "It's a dead end. I really can't see you working on an assembly line." Instantly I imagined working at a factory like Lavern and Shirley. It actually seemed like it might be fun.

"I wish we could afford for you to go to college," my mom said. I really wished I could go to college too, but there was absolutely no path for me to get to that point.

The next day, Mr. Brown, my drafting teacher, agreed to write me a recommendation and was very encouraging. I not only was in his drafting and architectural classes, I was also his teacher's aide for an extra period. Mr. Ochs also wrote a glowing recommendation in my favor. For the third one, I asked Mrs. Wooten. She was my favorite teacher. She taught Civics and World Problems.

"Absolutely not," she said when I told her about the program. I was a little shocked. She stood a few inches above me at 6'2" but seemed more like 7'. She was a former Vogue model in the 30s or 40s and had been some kind of United States ambassador to China or Japan in the late 50s for one of our presidents. As she stood in front of our class, I always imagined her in Japan, towering over the people like a giant in Gulliver's Travels—all the little people staring and moving out of her way. "You are going to college," she said sternly.

"My parents can't afford college," I said.

"Then you pay for it yourself," she said. "How hard is that?"

"How?"

"You will figure it out. You're a smart girl."

"What if I take this job and go to college too?"

Her bright orange lipstick moved into a smile. "Do you promise?"

"I promise," I said and I actually meant it. I did want to go to college. I wasn't sure exactly what I wanted to do, maybe be an architect or a journalist. I never really considered college so I never gave much thought to a major. I just needed money so I could move out and be on my own.

"I'm glad," she said and sat back down at her desk. "I was going to write you the letter anyway. But don't you forget, you promised."

I had my three letters and now just needed the final sign off from Principal Chapman, I took the paperwork to the office where the principal had to sign off before I could submit it. He was standing at the attendance desk, so I waved.

Mr. Chapman was a good looking black man. He always wore a suit and tie and you would never find him in his office because he was walking the halls or checking in on classes. It seemed like he knew every kid's name in the school. One time, when I was supposed to be in my typing class on the second floor but instead was walking down the hall on the first floor, skipping class, I ran into Mr. Chapman. He just shook his head and said, "If typing isn't your thing, you should withdraw so it doesn't go on your record."

"Good idea," I said with a shock as my face heated up. How on earth could he not only know I was skipping but that I was skipping Typing?

"I have some papers," I said.

He looked through the stack and quickly signed where he was supposed to without asking questions. "I am proud of you," he said looking up and smiling. It felt weird for him to say that. I felt my heart in my throat.

Several weeks later, I was called to Mr. Ochs office, where there was a man from Puget Sound Naval Shipyard waiting to interview me. It was game day, so I was wearing my cheerleading uniform, not an appropriate outfit for a job interview. I wished someone would have told me about the interview.

George Sumner was a medium built man who looked older than my dad. He could have been closer to my grandfather's age. He had thinning grey hair combed back across an obvious bald spot. He looked like he had a day's growth of beard, which made him appear a little sloppy, but he had a nice easy smile.

I sat across from him, easily answering the interview questions at the same time I kept pulling at my skirt, making sure it stayed in place. He asked me about my family and about school. We seemed to have a good rapport. He even said I reminded him of his granddaughter.

"I heard you got a job at the shipyard." Mike stopped in front of me, where I was sitting waiting for the bus to go home. He was wearing gold and black running shorts and a matching sleeveless shirt with Lincoln written across the front. He was such a cutie but so thin.

"I did," I said with a pretend shy smile.

"Congratulations." He sat next to me and we talked about life.

Mike was such a sweetheart. We had so much in common, we never ran out of things to say. He was not as shy as I always thought—he just let me talk and was a good listener. I started thinking I was in love with him.

He borrowed his parent's Volvo and we went out. I don't remember our first date, but I do remember uncomfortable sex in the front seat. He was the perfect guy, I really liked him. He was smart, funny and from a good family. He was a year older than me. I could imagine a white picket kind of life with him.

Mike left for the boot camp and I still had a year of high school. We wrote back and forth, missing each other. The plan was that he would go back to college after four years in the Marines and he would become a police officer. I would work at the shipyard and save enough money to also go to college. We would get married after college.

XII

1981 Charisse (Age 18)

Chapter 27

My dad drove me across the narrows bridge. It took us 45 minutes to reach the main gate of Puget Sound Naval Shipyard.

"Are you sure you want to do this?" my father asked.

"I'm sure," I said.

"I just can't see you in a factory job. You're a smart girl."

"It's not a factory. It's a shipyard."

"That's worse," he said.

"I'll be done at 4 o'clock. Can you pick me up?"

He pointed to the McDonalds on the corner. "I'll meet you there."

There was a line of kids that looked about my age so I walked over to them. "Is this the work study program?"

A tall, thin, dark-skinned young man nodded his head and smiled, so I took my place in line behind him. I was nervous and excited at the same time. We sat in meetings, filled out piles of paperwork, and were even examined by medical staff. It was a long, boring day but around 3 o'clock we were put into small groups.

There were five people in my group and we were greeted by George, the same guy who interviewed me. I was so relieved to see him again, I wanted to hug him. He took us up to the fifth floor of a tall office building, where we were again divided up and assigned to different departments. The sign on the wall just outside the elevator said 'Planning and Estimating'. As we made our way down the hall, he stopped, introduced one of the kids to a supervisor in an office of cubicles, then, down the hall further, another kid, another supervisor, until I was the only one left.

I was assigned to George's department. He was the manager of the whole floor, so he had a corner office with a large glass window overlooking the main street of the shipyard, which was like a small contained city with trucks full of equipment, giant cranes moving back and forth, forklifts laden with pallets of material, and people with different colored hardhats walking around with purpose.

George's department had representatives from every trade. They organized work for all the other sections on the floor. We had a structural guy, an electrical guy, an electronics guy, a sheet metal guy, a welding guy, a pipe fitting guy, a public works guy and a woodshop guy. The only other female was the secretary, Cindy. Cindy was just a few years older than me. Most of the guys in this department were as old as George or older.

I spent the next six weeks with these guys. They made sure I was well informed on how the shipyard worked, and each one of them took me into their field to tour the trade so I could have a better idea of what I wanted to pick for my trade. At the end of the work study program, I would have to pick three choices of trades I would pursue, either as an apprentice or as a helper.

I was assigned to the woodshop for my six-week tour of the shop. My supervisor was a handsome thirty-something guy with a great crew. Everyone took time to teach me some part of the trade. I got to work on boat repair, where we used epoxy and fiberglass cloth to repair small boats. It was fun and satisfying work even though you had to wear a facemask and white Tyvek coveralls that made you sweat.

I wasn't that good at the actual woodcraft, but I followed instructions well. I worked with Ralph. He was in his late 20s and had a giant beard and kind blue eyes. He was big and smelled like fresh cedar. I liked working with him.

The crew invited me to come to a party the following Saturday. Ralph said he would give me a ride, so I agreed. I was too naïve at the time to realize he liked me. I was still only 17, so I thought it was pretty cool to hang out with a bunch of adults. Ralph had already been married and divorced, but he didn't have any kids.

Ralph showed up to my parent's house on a Harley. He had big black boots on with a matching black leather jacket. He looked so dangerous, like a real biker. I smiled, wishing my dad was home.

"How old is this guy," my mother asked, looking out the window at him.

"Nineteen," I said quickly. "He looks a lot older because of his beard." I couldn't tell if she believed me or not—maybe she didn't care.

Ralph came up to the house and introduced himself to my mom before I could get him out of there. I wasn't sure if she bought the age, but she didn't push it and didn't stop me from getting on the bike. Ralph put a helmet on me and buckled it under my chin, then he held the bike steady as I climbed up behind him. I wasn't sure where to put my hands, so I held on to his waist. After some awkward jerking, he moved my hand so I was I was hugging his waist. I was as close as I could get, avoiding the wind. "Just lean with me," he said.

We showed up at Brian's and Darlene's house. They were married and both worked with us in the woodshop. It was so weird seeing all these people in their normal, everyday clothes talking about fishing, hunting, kids, and subjects I couldn't relate to, so I kept my mouth shut for the most part. Ralph was kind and attentive and kept me close, filling my glass when it needed it.

I came out of the restroom to find Ralph waiting for me. "Do you want to see Brian's Boston Whaler?"

"Uh…Sure…I guess." I had no idea what a Boston Whaler was, but Ralph took my hand and led me to the end of the hall where there was a door leading to a garage. Inside, there was a large fishing boat, a Boston Whaler.

"Isn't it gorgeous?" he said, putting a hand on the hull and then on my shoulder, "gorgeous like you?" I got what he was trying to say, but it felt weird to be compared to a boat. But he had me pinned, with his face so close I could feel his breath as he kissed me—very soft at first. He knew how to kiss and I got lost for a few minutes. Then a loud knock at the inside door made me jump and hit my lip on his tooth. He pushed back with a giant smile and a huge bulge in his pants. When he opened the door to go back in, everyone stood in the hall and started laughing.

"Oh, my God," I whispered. I was unbelievably embarrassed and could feel the stinging on my face where the beard had rubbed when we kissed.

For the next few weeks, I stayed weekends with Ralph and we drank Asti-Spumante and hung out with friends. He was so much older and more experienced, I felt like an adult.

I had turned 18 in November so when Cathy asked me to share an apartment with her, I was all in. She was a foster child, so at 18 she had to move out. I was just wanting to get out of my house, away from crazy rules and church. As soon as I started back in January at the shipyard, I packed up my car and moved from Tacoma to Bremerton, which shortened my commute from an hour to less than 15 minutes.

Cathy was a newly converted Mormon and I was currently considering becoming a Buddhist, so it was an odd partnership, but we both were smart enough not to let religion get in the way if we wanted to be able to live together. The only thing I really knew about Mormons was that you could have as many wives as you wanted and you had to get baptized for dead people. She did try to preach some Mormon values to me, but I had been trained by the Pentecostals on how to come back at Mormons. The Pentecost's believed the Mormon religion was a cult and vice versa. I decided the only way I could speak to her about anything was to read her books—the Latter-day Saint's version of the King James version of the bible and the Book of Mormon. I found it to be as ridiculous as the Pentecostal crap.

I loved every one of the trades I worked in. I really wanted the woodshop because the people who worked there had become my friends and I liked hanging out with them. They treated me like an adult. Everyone was so nice, but "my guys" in the Code talked me into picking the electronics apprenticeship because it had the most college credits and you worked 90 percent of the time inside the shop. I had a bunch of fathers in that office, but I loved it because they actually cared about me.

Chapter 28

Working in the electronic shop was a perfect fit for my skills. I worked in the graphics section, where I was able to use my graphic arts and design experience. We made metal labels for electronic equipment and printed circuit boards. I learned how to solder and I got to build my own Fluke Multi-meter with a Heath kit. One of the other students I worked with was a good-looking guy, David. He was from Rodgers High School in North Tacoma. I liked to hear his laugh.

"Would you go to my senior prom with me?" I asked him without really thinking about it. Mike was gone and it was my senior year. It would be the last high school event where I would be able to see all my friends I had missed that year.

"Sure," he said. I was actually surprised that he agreed to go with me. He seemed kind of shy, but he was cute. I loved his smile. I didn't consider this a real date, but David took it very seriously and made sure I had a good time.

David actually took the extra effort to get a light blue tux that matched perfectly with my light blue formal. He took me to a real steak and lobster dinner before the dance. David's brother got us some alcohol and we drank Vodka and Mountain Dew even before we walked into the dance. I probably drank a little too much and we only stayed long enough for pictures and a few dances. I took my shoes off and hid them under the curtains of the venue. I didn't like being taller than him. I was too drunk to go home, so I stayed the night with him. I brought clothes to change into in case we went somewhere after the prom. We went to his house. He was living with his brother but no one was there when we got there, so we just went into David's bedroom. I felt so bad that I didn't really remember having sex with him, but I was sure I did. I prayed out loud all the way home. Again, I prayed, "Please god, don't let me be pregnant, I promise I will never do that again."

Both David and I were hired as apprentices in the electronics department. There were only six coveted spots. We were constantly reminded how special we were. I was embarrassed at how much of a slut I had been, sleeping with him on our first and only date. I didn't know how to act, so I pretty much ignored David at work, and he pretty much went on with his life and dated some of the next class of work studies that started working at the shipyard.

Mike came home after his six weeks of boot camp and stayed with me at my apartment. I thought I was in love with this guy before he left for the Marines, but the tall, thin young man had transformed into a tall muscular man with a high and tight haircut and the same beautiful blue eyes with curly lashes. I couldn't help getting butterflies whenever he was near me. I was sure he was the one and I was sure he felt the same way.

He spent almost the whole time he was home with me, disappointing his parents, but we had to make the most of our short time together. I was so depressed when he left for South Carolina. I felt like I had a hole right in the middle of my stomach. I carried around a picture of him dressed in his uniform in a small pouch with my shipyard identification badge. I looked at that picture 50 times a day and kissed his cute face.

It was the first week of our actual apprenticeship training. We spent eight hours a day learning how to solder on circuit boards. I had already spent time in that section, so I was way ahead of the class and could get my project done in half the time, which was good because all day I felt sick and had to run to the restroom every few hours. I couldn't keep anything down, but there was no way I could call in sick in my first week, so I suffered through it.

"Are you okay," Lea asked. Lea was one of the few women who worked at the shipyard. She was a few years older than me and had spent four years in the military. She had already been married and divorced. I worked with her for a few weeks when I was assigned to her section as a work study. We hit it off and I liked hanging out with her.

"I think I have the flu," I said. I came out of the toilet and rinsed my mouth out in the sink.

"You look pretty pale." She put her hand on my forehead. "No fever. If you need to go to the doctor, let me know. I drove in today," she said. I just nodded.

After lunch, Lea poked her head into the work area we were working in. "You okay?" she mouthed.

I nodded my head slowly, but I still felt like crap. She saw that our instructor was busy across the room, so she came over to me with a small piece of paper.

"Here is a doctor with an office just a few blocks away. I will go with you if you want." I took the paper, and after the next trip to the bathroom, I made the call. I was able to get in the next afternoon.

The doctor's office was a surprisingly old building. I felt like I just walked back in time. We sat in uncomfortable chairs that might have come out of my grandmother's kitchen. It didn't take long before I was taken back to the exam room and the doctor came in with a clipboard. They took blood and had me pee in a cup.

The next morning, I received a call at work. It was the nurse from the old doctor's office. "Congratulations, you are pregnant."

"Okay, thanks," I said flatly and hung up the phone. The blood rushed to my head and I felt like I was going to faint. There was no way I could be pregnant—except for the fact I had never used any form of birth control. Besides, the doctor who took out my ovary when I was 15 said I probably couldn't get pregnant.

What was I going to say to Mike? Was he going to be excited to be a father or mad. How was I going to tell my parents?

That night I called Mike. He was on the East Coast, so it was late and I woke him up. I told him what I was doing at work and he was telling me what he was doing. Somewhere in the middle of all that, I blurted out, "You're going to be a dad." The phone went silent. "Are you mad?"

"No, I'm not mad," he said. "More like shock. I am not sure what to say. What do you want to do?" Now it was my turn to be silent.

"I don't know," I said. Until this moment, there was only one choice and that was to have a baby. Could I get an abortion? I didn't think I could. "I don't know," I said, again feeling so sad.

"Do you want to get married?"

"Are you asking?"

"Did you want me to?"

"Oh, my God, NO! I mean I don't know. I didn't do this on purpose to trap you." I felt flush. Is that what he was thinking? "I don't need to get married. I can do this on my own. I have a good job."

"Can you keep your job if you're pregnant?"

"I think so."

"We can still get married when I get out," he said.

"Okay. I've got to go," I said, but I needed to get off the phone because I was going to fall apart. The conversation didn't go anything like I planned.

At work the next day, Lea came and asked me what happened. I told her about the conversation.

"It sounds like he wants to marry you."

"I am not forcing anyone to marry me."

"Can you do this on your own?"

"Of course, I can." I was never so unsure of anything in my life.

My mom was in the upstairs bathroom brushing her hair. I stood in the open door watching her. "Mom, I have something to tell you." I was getting sick to my stomach and I could feel the blood leave my brain.

There must have been something in my voice, because she stopped mid brush and turned towards me. "What is wrong?"

"I…well you…I.?"

"What happened?" She started getting that panicky voice that came just before a breakdown, so I just spit it out.

"You are going to be a grandma." I shut my eyes as tight as I could, waiting for a scream or crying or some kind of violent reaction but nothing happened. I opened my eyes and she was smiling, not only smiling, but like winning the lottery smiling.

"Are you getting married?" She was so excited, I thought she would start jumping up and down any second. This was the opposite of what I thought would be her reaction.

"I don't know," I said.

Later that evening, Mike called and said his sister was willing to pay for an abortion. She would even go with me if I needed someone to drive. I hung up. I don't think I had ever felt so sad and lonely. He tried to call back several times but I didn't answer. It was a few days later that I answered the phone and he told me that he wasn't telling me to get an abortion and that he had told his parents. They were very upset, but they were willing to drive me across country so we could get married in South Carolina. I told him that I would let him know the next day.

I sat with Lea at lunch and she convinced me that it would probably be the best idea to move. I agreed and finally felt a little relief that I had made a decision.

Before I left, I found out Lea had taken my place in the apprenticeship. Afterword, I wondered if she knew that if I quit she would get my place. Either way, I did the right thing.

1956: Bernice Lucille (Age 12)

"Am I adopted?" Bernice asked her Grandma Clara. Bernice spent a lot of time at her grandmother's house, which was right next door. Grandma was the only source of sanity in her life. Her mom and dad were constantly fighting.

"No. Don't be silly," she said. "I was there at your birth."

"I feel like I am so different from my family."

"You are not like those people?"

"My mom?"

"No, you are not like her?" Clara shook her head, thinking it was probably her fault Nelda was like she was. She didn't have the energy to control her and just let her do whatever she wanted. Even the few times she had tried to discipline her, Nelda had run to Charlie, who could not say no to her.

"Who am I like?"

"You are like your father." Clara liked George. He was a good looking, polite young man. She had hoped Nelda would settle down when she married him.

"Elmer?"

"No, George White," she said firmly.

"My mom said George is not my father. I asked my dad Elmer if he was my father and he said ask my mom. My mom said no. When I asked her who my real father was, she said she isn't going to tell me because I would look for him and he didn't know about me."

"That is not true. George White is your father. You look just like him."

"I hate him." Bernice didn't know why she said it, maybe it was to satisfy her mother, who wanted her to hate him.

"Why do you hate him?"

"I don't know, I just do."

"Why don't you write him a letter and tell him how you feel."

Bernice wrote George a long letter and mailed it. Just writing it made her feel so much better even though she still wasn't sure he really was her dad. George was living in Oregon when he got the letter. He called Nelda and she didn't hang up on him but invited him up to see his daughter since Elmer was currently serving a little time in the County Jail. A few weeks later George came to see Bernice.

Bernice was nervous seeing her dad. She had met him when she was a lot younger when he had come to visit. Her mother actually asked him to come. She was in a fight with Elmer and was staying with her sister Marion. Bernice remembered that he had brought her a beautiful doll and brought her sister and cousin rubber balls. As soon as her father had left, her mother took the doll right out of her hands and gave it to her cousin. "He is not your dad," she said.

This time George brought her a pair of earrings made from Myrtle wood. Bernice held them tightly in her hand. She would hide them from her mother so she wouldn't take them away from her. The next time Bernice would see George was when she turned 18 and would get on a bus and travel to Portland to see him. Bernice knew that it was best not to even mention her father's name or suffer the wrath of Nelda.

Chapter 29

I pulled up to the house on 84th Street and Josette was standing out on the front porch. She saw my car and was at the sidewalk as I pulled up. She got in and we drove in silence. She was wondering what was going on and I was wondering how I was going to tell her.

We stopped at A&W, ordered ice cream floats and sat across from each other in the booth. I looked into her light brown eyes. She was so grown up—a teenager now. It was hard to believe. "I'm leaving," I said.

"You already left," she said. I had moved into my own apartment during my senior year not long after I turned 18. I had finished all my required classes and was in a full-time work study program at Puget Sound Naval Shipyard, and a part time job at Mr. Steak. I had finished all my required classes and graduated a few weeks before.

"I'm moving to South Carolina," I said

"Where is South Carolina?" She didn't look happy.

"It's on the East Coast somewhere." I wasn't exactly sure where, but I knew it was across the country.

"You cannot leave." She started to cry.

"I'm pregnant." She stopped crying and dropped the spoon that she had been digging into the root beer, pulling out vanilla ice cream. It landed with a plop on the table, making a mess. I felt so bad. I didn't want to leave my sisters but I needed to get away. I needed to have a life away from all the crazy of my life.

"We can write all the time. I will come home when I can. I promise." I could tell she was trying to act happy for me, but she was so sad. "You will be okay. I promise." I was promising things I had no idea if I could control.

I moved all my things from my apartment back to my parent's house. I would only bring my clothes. I gave Josette most of the clothes I would leave behind.

I even left my car for my dad to sell. My car was my pride and joy. It was a 1969 Green VW Bug. Uncle Hector knew I was looking for a car and his friend had one for sale so he took me to look at it. I wanted it. My dad said, "You are not getting a Volkswagen. They are death machines. You get in a wreck and they crush like a tin can." I bought it anyway. I was 18 and had my own money.

Mike's parents were proud Norwegians with family that had immigrated to this country just a few generations back. They were very traditional and were almost as old as my grandparents. Mike said he was "an accident". He was born when they were in their 40s. My mom was only 38 and she was about to be a grandmother. Both Norbert and Vivian had white hair and looked their age. They were very nice and took the news that their son was going to be a father fairly well. At least in front of me, they handled it well. They even volunteered to drive me across country to get married and help us settle in.

XIII

1982: Charisse (Age 19)

Chapter 30

The Ellington's showed up at my parent's house to load me up on our road trip across the country. I invited them in to introduce my parents. The house was a split level so we had to walk up a short flight of steps to get to the living room. Mr. Ellington instantly held out his hand to greet my parents but we all froze as Vivian started to cry. Huge tears ran down her face as she stared at my father.

"I'm so sorry." She pulled a handkerchief out of her sweater pocket and wiped her tears and blew her nose. She gained her composure and then, instantly, like nothing had happened, greeted my parents.

Later, when I talked to Mike, he told me that his mom was worried about our children. If they were "mixed" race, they might have a harder time in life. I guess I never told him I wasn't of mixed race. "My sisters don't have problems," I said.

"They are just old fashioned," he said. I was conflicted on whether I should reveal my DNA secret to make them feel better or keep it safe inside. I never told anyone about my father and pretended all these years to be Mexican so I could keep my family together. I wanted my sisters to stay my sisters. I didn't want to be different.

We moved into a single wide mobile home on Palmetto Circle that Mike's parents had bought for us. We paid Mike's parents $200 a month with interest. It was like we were purchasing our first home. Overall the neighborhood was pretty quiet. The mobile home park was actually a part of the base, so all our neighbors were also Marine Corps families. About a week after I moved in, the next-door neighbor invited me over for coffee. She was a tiny thing, not even five feet tall, slim with very light blonde hair and vivid blue eyes. She looked like a child with an older woman's face. She smoked a lot, so she had a raspy voice.

I walked into the smoke-filled trailer and held my breath. I was pregnant and I didn't want to poison my baby. There were two other neighbor ladies sitting in the living room, coffee in hands. I was definitely the young one and felt awkward as a new wife just a few months pregnant.

"Have a seat," a bigger lady said, pointing to an empty seat near her. I sat on the edge. The television was on and there was a soap opera, maybe *One Life to Live*. It seemed too early for soap operas, but the East Coast was weird anyway. It was also too loud and the woman had to talk really loud. Two of the three were smoking. Again, I tried to avoid the smoke so my baby wouldn't be exposed.   They all introduced themselves and said where they lived in the circle. It apparently was a tight-knit community where everyone knew everything about their neighbors. Most of the husbands worked together in some manner. My husband was Military Police for the Air Station less than a mile away. The neighbors to my right and the husband of the blonde were both Marine Drill Sergeants working at Paris Island. They worked on me for at least an hour, milking all the details they could out of me so they had some new juicy conversation when I left. I knew what they were doing, so I just gave them enough to be interesting.

According to this group, there were only two officers in our neighborhood, and they aren't allowed to fraternize with us or our husbands, who were enlisted. I knew a little about rank from my time working for the Navy, and I wasn't intimidated by the whole rank system. I wasn't in the Marines. They soon got bored with me and moved on.

They seemed comfortable enough with me that one of the ladies pulled a big black dildo out of her purse.

"Look what I got," she said to the group. I was in shock but acted like I saw this kind of thing every day.

Being born and raised in the Pacific Northwest, I had never seen a cockroach, so when I saw my first one it was a shock. I screamed loud, causing Mike to run in like something bad was happening. He smashed it with a shoe. The next morning, there was a water bug, a cockroach on steroids, in the bathtub. Mike wasn't home so I called him at work and he sent one of the guys who were currently driving through the neighborhood. I felt stupid sitting on the front deck. South Carolina had too many bugs. For the next two years, I slept with my feet tucked up, away from the bottom of the bed, and shook out all my shoes before I put them on.

Bugs were not all that was wrong with Beaufort. Tornadoes were a real concern. I found out why our mobile home had long metal strips tied down on both sides to keep it in place when one night the wind shook our home so hard the closet doors all flew open and dishes came out of the cupboards.

Chapter 31

It was late evening and Mike just got home from working swing shift. He had taken off his boots but was still in his camo's sitting on the couch with the TV on. I tried to stay awake so I could see him when he got home. I would try to make some food he would like but I wasn't a good cook and we didn't have a lot of money to spend on food. I couldn't find a job until after I had the baby.

I was having some weird pains in my back and my stomach. I went into the bathroom and sat on the toilet. I felt a warm sensation and looked down and saw the toilet filling with blood. "Oh, my God!" I yelled. I didn't know what to do so I stood up and watched the blood run down my leg and was now creating a small puddle on the floor.

"Oh Shit," Mike said. He grabbed a towel and put it on the ground. "Where is that coming from?"

"I don't know," I said, crying.

"We need to go to the hospital." He was now very calm. He handed me a towel and said to put it between my legs. He slipped on his boots without tying them. He got me a robe and led me to the car, carrying more towels that he laid out on the seats.

He sped out of our community onto the main highway until a local police officer pulled him over. He explained the situation so the police officer had us follow him with his lights and siren blasting. We got to the hospital but it was not the military hospital so they turned us away and we drove a few more miles to the Naval Hospital, where I was treated for a miscarriage. The blood had stopped flowing and I was confused and didn't know what to do. I couldn't stop crying. Mike was the one that held it together and calmly handled everything. He asked all the questions and got me back in the car. It felt like it took forever to get home. The whole time, I cried, not only for the baby that I had lost, but for quitting my job, moving across the country so far away from my family. I felt so alone.

The next day, Mike took me to the Naval Hospital where I was expecting them to suck out all the remnants of my baby, but instead the doctor said, "you're still pregnant."

"How can that be?" I said. "There was so much blood."

"It's possible that you were pregnant with twins," he said. "I clearly hear a healthy heartbeat, and I would guess early February for delivery. You have a tipped uterus but nothing that will stop you from a normal delivery."

I was excited but exhausted. I had not slept the night before. Mike took me home and went back to work and left me alone. I sat in the middle of the kitchen floor and broke down. Tears ran down my face and I would have screamed but the neighbors would hear. I was an emotional wreck and desperately needed to talk to my mother.

We didn't have any extra money but at this point I was willing to pay the exorbitant long distance rates to talk to my mom. I dialed the number and got a message that the number had been disconnected. I tried again in case I dialed it wrong and got the same message. I waited a few minutes and tried again. I called the number more than ten times, but no one answered. I was alone. It was almost a month later when my mother finally called. She had received the letter I had written telling her the due date and a list of names I was considering.

Somehow my mom and dad found the money so my mom could be with me for the birth of my first child, her first grandchild. She was happy and excited to be a grandmother even though she was only 39 years old. She came on February 1st. My official due date was February 6th. Mom said you never know, because all her babies came early. I was huge and had gained 69 pounds.

I finally went into labor February 19th but didn't deliver the baby until almost 20 hours later. This child was in no rush. He was breech, so all the labor pains didn't really hurt. The doctor finally decided the only way we were going to get this kid out was through a cesarean section. He was a healthy 8 pounds, 11 ounces and 22 inches long. When my mom first saw him, she said, "He looks just like your dad."

I was a little bit out of it because of all the drugs they had given me, because I thought she said the baby looked like my dad.

"What?"

"He looks just like your dad." She saw my confusion. "Your biological dad."

"Oh."

XIV

1983: Charisse (Age 20)

Chapter 32

Matt was 8 months old when I finally came home for Teresa's wedding. My dad's janitorial business was doing well, so they had moved to a nice house on Forrest Hill Lane in South Hill Puyallup. Lisa was going to Bates Vocational School in downtown Tacoma and still lived at home. Josette and Angelique were both struggling to get through high school. The problem was that my parents didn't put much value in education, especially if you were a girl, so the girls didn't have to go if they didn't want to. It was hard enough to fit into a group, but because they were Pentecostal, they stuck out like sore thumbs and people tended to shy away from the religious freaks.

Teresa and Joe had been dating since she was 15, so we all knew they would eventually get married.

"I wish Christopher could have stayed for the wedding," Josette said.

"Who is Christopher?" I asked.

Josette looked confused. "He is our brother."

"We don't have a brother." I said. "Is it someone from church?" I assumed that Christopher must be some teenager my parents took a liking to and he called them mom and dad so my younger sisters might call him their brother.

"He's a real brother," Lisa said. "We met him at the family reunion."

"What family reunion? Nobody told me anything about this."

"We went to Texas for a family reunion and Christopher was there. Dad had gotten some lady pregnant, and they had a baby but didn't get married. Chris's aunt adopted him, and he didn't know he had a dad until Uncle Cruz told him. They were playing on the same baseball team. Isn't that weird. Definitely a small world." Lisa, spit it all out like it was no big deal.

"He was just here a few weeks ago." Josette said.

"Here?" I said. "Mom didn't care?"

Apparently, Uncle Cruz thought it would be fun to surprise my dad with his son in front of the entire family. I didn't even know they all went to Texas. I felt like I wasn't part of this family. All this time wanting a boy, my dad already had a secret son.

"Jesus Christ, I've only been gone for 14 months," I said out loud.

Like on cue, my parents walked into the kitchen where all us girls were sitting around the table. "So, it's okay for you to know your son but I can't know my father? Thanks a lot." I picked up my son and walked out. I was furious and I could feel my face burning. All these years feeling guilty that I even wanted to meet my biological father, and everyone just accepted this new kid into their lives.

XV

1984: Charisse (Age 21)

Chapter 33

Mike got orders to Okinawa, Japan for the next two years, so we decided I should move back to Washington to be close to my family.

We found a small house in the South side of Tacoma, not too far from the neighborhood where we both grew up. We had a little money for a down payment since we sold our mobile home in Beaufort and had paid Mike's parents back. I was going to try to get my job back at the shipyard so he could go to college when he got out in less than two years.

My mom and dad were going through another transition. They lost their house when one of my dad's church friends stole his money, his work truck and his cleaning equipment. The guy was in charge of the "books" and never paid the IRS, so he was facing a lot of financial challenges.

Josette and Angelique moved in with Teresa, who had just found out she was pregnant. Lisa stayed with me for a few days until she took an apartment downtown at the mortuary. It was free rent for answering the phones and dispatching the guys to go pick up bodies in the middle of the night. Our parents lived in a pop-up tent trailer on the church property. They had no phone, no electricity, no water and no bathroom. It seemed like it didn't really bother my parents. My mom still looked well put together every time you saw her. One thing I can say about them is that they were survivors.

Now that I was back home with my son and my husband was overseas, I had time to think about my biological father again. I took my son with me to the public library downtown where there was a full set of phonebooks from every county of every state. I pulled out a few of the books and looked up the name "McFarlane" but found there were other ways to spell it. "McFarlin" was less common but I knew I had to include it.

I copied addresses until my hand hurt. I bet I had close to fifty. I made 50 copies of a letter I had written, explaining that I was searching for my biological father. I said his name was Gene or Eugene and he was stationed at Fort Lewis in 1963, when I was born. I held my breath as I let the batch fall into the post box nearest to the library, hoping that one of the addressees would recognize Gene and write me back. I hopelessly checked the mail every day for a month, and I had almost given up any hope when I finally received the letter from my biological grandmother, Lila McFarlin. A few days later, I got a letter from my real father.

It took a long time to get here, five and a half hours by plane and years of anticipation. I never imagined I would actually meet my biological father, but here I was, minutes away. I held on to Matt, who was waking up in my lap. His little face was so sweet— his soft lips and pudgy red cheeks. I don't think I had ever felt this kind of love before. He had my heart. Would my own father have this feeling for me and his grandson? We didn't even know each other. My life has been filled with lies, deceit, and denial, and all I wanted was to move, to live, to solve this mystery that was my life. Who am I? Where do I belong? Do I belong? Anywhere? The anticipation was almost too much. What was I going to say? Would I recognize him because of that parent-child bond?

It was a rough landing. I held on to my small boy and the older, well-dressed gentleman seated next to me put out a protective arm across my son and me. The man was a handsome older gentleman with black hair with silver highlights. His blue eyes sparkled when he smiled. He said his name was Jim. He had been so kind during the flight. He had even reached out with his large man hands and easily held Matthew when I had to use the restroom. For a minute, I imagined that he was my father and we were flying together to our extended family in Milwaukee.

"Are you visiting family?" he asked me early in the flight.

"Yes," I answered, "My father."

"That is great," he said, then spoke to my son. "I bet you are excited to see your grandpa." His deep voice had changed to light and soft when he spoke to Matthew.

"Are you going to see family?" I asked.

"No," he said, "business."

I didn't know what to say, but I felt sad for him, so I just half smiled and hugged my baby.

Matthew smiled, showing off his little white baby teeth like he always did. He was the sweetest baby. His smile mesmerized even the grumpiest people. Everyone wanted to hold him, even the checker at the grocery store would ask to hold him and delay the line, but nobody ever cared, they would just smile and wave and say goo-goo sounds to him. It was like he was a magic baby, he seldom cried. Sometimes I was afraid someone would steel him since he was not afraid of strangers.

I walked in slow motion, my heart beating out of my chest, down the breezeway of the General Mitchel International Airport, surrounded by my fellow travelers who rushed by, finally freed from the constraints of their seatbelts. The airport was so hot inside the windows had fogged up, isolating us from a bitter cold awaiting outside. Matt hung onto my neck as I balanced him on my hip. Even though he was only a year and a half, he was the size of a three-year-old. He was heavy and I was tired.

I could finally see where the invisible security line held back the greeting public. I saw Jim walk towards the drivers holding placards with names written, boldly signaling their fare. I watched him as he froze in front of the placard that said, "J. Williams". He turned around, scanned the crowd until he saw me, stopped, smiled and gave me a big thumb's up.

Families were reunited, with the fathers and mothers carrying balloons and flowers. People laughed, cried, hugged, creating a bit of chaos which made me a little uneasy. How would I recognize my own father? How would I react? How would he react and how would I respond?

The only photograph I had ever seen was one my grandmother had sent me. It was an 8x10 blown up, grainy image of Gene in full camouflage standing next to a slaughtered deer hanging upside down with its guts hanging out. Nothing in that picture would help me identify him today.

Finally, I spotted a man standing away from the crowd, hands deep in his pockets, looking straight at me with a smile. He looked like an average guy, one you might run into at the local bar. He was close to six feet tall with thick brown hair. His well-worn jeans were too big and were fringed at the bottom, exposing heavy work boots. He wore a white t-shirt under a blue flannel. He held a military type overcoat under one arm. He smiled and I knew I found my father. I fought tears as I moved towards him.

People continued to walk past us as we awkwardly hugged a greeting, not understanding what a momentous occasion they were witnessing—a father and daughter meeting for the first time.

I wanted to cry out "Daddy," but he was a stranger. I wasn't really convinced he was happy to see me. The years of searching, hoping, praying for this moment threatened my composure, but I held strong. I was touching him and he was touching me. "Why did you leave me? Why didn't you save me?" I said without a voice. My voice left me a long time ago.

I searched his face as if something would trigger a memory from babyhood. Some recognition that bonded us from birth. What I saw was his eyes. One eye was the exact light blue as mine but the other eye was different. Three quarters of it was the same blue and a quarter of it was brown. It reminded me of a marble I found as a kid. It was blue with a light brown streak through it. My daughter was born the following spring with the same mismatched eyes as her grandfather.

He had a nice smile and a kind face. I set my son down to give my arms a break. I was suddenly feeling overwhelmed. Was I happy, disappointed, or was it a combination of the excitement of my first plane ride and the strain of hauling an 18-month-old around all day? In any case, the surge of adrenaline was making me weak.

"I am happy I finally found you," I said, remembering all the times I planned ways I might find him.

"You have no idea how happy I am, girl." He smiled and the words filled my soul.

The airport in Milwaukee was much smaller than the one in Seattle. The car was parked right outside, which was a good thing. It was freezing. I was used to 50 degrees and the constant drizzle of the Pacific Northwest, so my first breath of below zero air was a shock. It was like we were in a dream. Piles of snow that lined the streets absorbed the normal traffic noise. A few cars had chains shackled to their tires and sounded like prisoners being led down the street. The buildings in Milwaukee were worn out, built mostly of brick with no real differentiating features. Some were just bigger than others. The largest were working factories billowing steam or black smoke into the freezing air.

He opened the passenger side door of a light blue two-door 1978 Thunderbird and I slid into the frozen seat. There was no car seat for my son so I held him in my lap buckling the seat belt across us both.

The first thing I noticed about the apartment were the books. I had never seen so many books outside of a library. There was a wall of shelves where books were stacked so full they spilled out to the floor in front of the shelves and even took up all of what could have been a dining room table. I was the only person in my family who loved to read—I must have inherited the love of reading from this man.

The furniture was well used and nothing really matched. There was a Lazy Boy chair with an arm repaired with duct tape in the center of the room—obviously where Gene spent most of his time. There was a TV tray on one side and a bedroom type end table on the other. The TV tray held a paperback and a Miller Light can. The end table had a TV guide and an overflowing ashtray. The whole room reminded me of my grandparent's house back home with the cigarette smoke and stale alcohol.

The bathroom was small and thick with the strong smell of soap. The toilet had been cleaned but was stained black.

We talked until late in the night while Matt slept on the couch near me. Gene told me about his childhood on the farm being the eldest of ten kids, his job and his last marriage.

"I was in the Army stationed at Fort Lewis when we met. Your ma was a beautiful girl but very naïve." He smiled at the memory as I took every word in. "I remember she went on television and sang 'Aunt Nothing but A Hound Dog'. I believe it was directed at me." He laughed, which started a coughing attack.

My mom sang on TV? I couldn't imagine the mother of my youth—who was always so emotional and stressed out—as a singer. "I was pretty angry at her for keeping you a secret all these years," I said.

"We were very young and I wasn't too excited about getting married, but I was also not too excited about going to jail either." He told me that in those days in the Army, my choice was getting locked up or marriage. He laughed. "Your ma was getting pretty big when we drove all the way to Idaho because they didn't have the three-day waiting period to get married. I was scared the whole time she might go into labor."

My grandmother Nelda drank quite a bit and during one of her drunken states she called me to tell me that my "real" father was a no-good piece of shit who tried to kill my mother and that is why they never told me about him. It was for my own safety. "My grandmother told me that you came to see me and tried to strangle my mom," I said.

"Jesus H, I would never have hurt your ma. The last time I saw your ma is when I showed up at your grandparent's house to see my kid and they threw me out. Your grandmother came out of the trailer in a bra holding a shotgun to my chest. I wasn't about to stick around. Your ma stood behind her and I could see her belly sticking out, very pregnant. I knew it wasn't mine, but we were still married. If I could have got my hands around anybody's neck, it would have been the no-good son of a bitch that knocked her up, my buddy, John. I was sure he was the one responsible. I wasn't the greatest guy back then. I couldn't take that rain," he said. "It just never stopped. I need four seasons."

"Seattle has been blamed for suicidal depression because of its grey skies and constant rain, but was it so bad you would leave your child?" I couldn't believe the words just left my brain and out of my mouth.

"I'm so sorry." Gene looked down for a second before he raised his head and looked me right into my blue eyes.

The next day I met Shane. He was fourteen, tall and thin with black hair. I had a brother. Shane had just recently been introduced to Gene. Even though they lived in the same town, they never met. Gene was married to another woman when Shane was conceived.
Sharon, the boy's mother, thought that it was best she didn't tell anyone who Shane's father was. The story was all too familiar. Shane grew up with a different man's name on his birth certificate. It was after the divorce that Sharon decided to tell Shane about his father, who had also gotten a divorce. Gene had two children who hadn't even known about him now in the same room. He looked happy.

We traveled two hours to Montello to the family farm where we would meet the family. Grandma and Grandpa McFarlin were both very large people. Grandma Lila was just like I expected. She had very few pictures of Gene or the family because of a house fire years before. She did give me a photograph of her holding my father. I looked like her and my son looked just like my father.

The family was so big that Thanksgiving was held at a community center that had a full kitchen. I met some aunts and uncles and a lot of cousins. One of my aunts was only a few years older than me and everyone thought we looked like sisters. Looking around the room I could see the resemblance. I finally looked like a family. The color of my eyes, the shape of my eyebrows, and definitely my nose. I had people.

Honestly, it wasn't all I expected and dreamed of. I thought Gene was going to be a business man with a big house. He would show me the room he had decorated and kept just in case he could have found me. He would have a stack of birthday cards he couldn't send but would buy and save for when he found me. But I am not sure he thought about me very much over the years. I thought there would be a lot more fuss over me, but I was just another addition to a huge family but I was part of this family. I am not saying that my father wasn't happy to meet me because I truly believed he was but if it wasn't for my effort, I wouldn't have ever met him.

I sat on the plane going back to my crazy life with my beautifully dysfunctional family. I held on to my young son and I decided that I would tell him about David.